2007

The American Frontier

This volume is one of a series of in-depth studies in United States History. For a complete description see page 241

2008

Consulting Editors

Alfred T. Clark, Jr.
  Los Angeles City Schools
John Hope Franklin
  University of Chicago
Anthony J. Petrillo
  Jefferson County Public Schools, Colorado
Ernest R. May
  Harvard University

The American Frontier

D. Duane Cummins

William Gee White

BENZIGER BROTHERS
NEW YORK
1968

Cover Illustration
Courtesy American Heritage Publishing Co., Inc.

First Edition, 1968
© Copyright 1968 Benziger Brothers, Inc.
All rights reserved.
Library of Congress Catalog Number 68-14972
Manufactured in the United States of America

Sincere appreciation to

B. B. Beard

whose love and affection
for the "Old West" have
been a constant inspiration.

CONTENTS

Introduction

One of the problems in the study of American frontier history is the dualism of *romance* and *reality*. There are many historians who argue that the great value of the frontier to America is as a myth or a symbol. That a nation profits from its myths is undeniable, but it is the opinion of the authors of this volume that a scholarly investigation of the American West is equally valuable.

There is no area of the country with a history more interesting and more distorted in the public mind than the American West. The struggles of the pioneer American to conquer the last frontier have caught and retained the imagination of the public to such an extent that a veritable mythology

1

has developed around the old west until dreams and reality have became all but indistinguishable. I would not deny Hollywood the income nor the public the recreation of the myth of the "Wild West", but I believe that we also deserve a factual history on which we can build and maintain the richly deserved respect and admiration for the truly great feat of developing the west.[1]

In any case, it doesn't matter if the West is considered as a myth, symbol or historic reality—the fact remains that important areas of American culture including the film industry, television, opera, Broadway, literature, music, art and even sports have all felt the impact of the frontier. Social scientists often interpret this frontier impact on American culture as a desire of the people to escape from the complexities of the twentieth century. Certain historians, however, suggest that the American frontier created unique traits which penetrated into American society, thereby causing the frontier to be an important stylist of a distinctive American character.

The word frontier has been used to describe a variety of things—a variety so large that historians have never been able to arrive at a fixed definition of the term. A frontier can mean a place, a process, a direction, a geographic expanse, a cultural region, a stable boundary or a moving, shifting, progressive line. The American frontier, as defined by America's most famous frontier authority, Frederick Jackson Turner, is a *process*—more specifically, a process of Americanization. This concept will be more thoroughly developed in subsequent chapters. It must also be recognized that the American frontier is often thought of as a fluid line moving progressively westward. One pioneer, Eleutheros Cooke, delivering an address at Norwalk, Ohio, in 1857, described the West in the following words:

And where is the West? Who shall fix its limits?

[1] McGee, Senator Gale, *The American West Magazine,* Vol. I, No. 1 (flyleaf) 1964.

. . . Two hundred years ago, to the Eastern continent, it held its court upon the Atlantic shore of
the New World; fifty years ago, Ohio was called
the *far* West; and it may now be properly defined
to mean that point where the savage and the white
man hold disputed sway.[2]

The terms West and frontier are often used interchange-
ably in the history of America. One is not any less difficult
to define than the other, and historians continually differ in
their interpretations.

A candidate for a degree in biology was asked to
differentiate between a frog and a toad. It did not
ease the student's cerebral embarrassment when,
after prolonged silence, the examiner, a product
of western perversity, told him not to worry because any country boy could describe the difference if someone needed to know. Such is the short-
coming of an academic approach to Reality.
Scholars quibble over definitions of the West while
laymen take the term for granted. The West is the
West, as even a fool knows. It is a place where
the cowhand puts his foot on a rail instead of his
rump on a stool, where the sheriff tacks up a leaf-
let offering REWARD for the desperado who
swaggers up, rips it down, laughs scornfully, and
rides off into the scenery.[3]

The term west is most frequently used to identify the direction of the frontier movement. Many nations have experienced a frontier movement, but not all of them moved in a
westward direction.

It should not be assumed that the term frontier applies

[2] From *A Nation Moving West* (p. 2) by Robert Richmond and
Robert Mardock. (By permission of University of Nebraska Press,
© 1966.)
[3] Ulph, Owen, "Literature and the American West," *The American
West* Magazine, p. 9.

only to America, or that the experience of a frontier movement was enjoyed solely by the United States. Emerson Hough once wrote that, "The Frontier knows no Country; it lies also in other lands and in other times than our own." Walter Prescott Webb, a widely known frontier historian, argues that the existence of a world frontier since 1500—and its settlement by European nations—is one of the important keys in understanding our modern civilization. Many historians have continually pointed to the significant parallels and contrasts to be drawn from a comparative study of the frontier experience in the United States with the frontier experiences in other historical societies.

The frontier process proved very useful to the historian, Paul MacKendrick, in his analysis of the expansion of ancient Rome. He observed a number of similarities to the American experience such as the geography of expansion, the type of settlements and settlers, and the influence which this experience had upon the central government. MacKendrick even compares the Roman political statesmen Cato and Marius with Lincoln and Jackson—all products of a frontier process.

A noted Russian historian, A. Lobanov-Rostovsky, describes the history of Russia within the framework of an eastward expansion. Lobanov-Rostovsky points to a number of parallels with the American frontier experience. Both countries were moving toward the Pacific Ocean and both of them contained an important geographic feature—the Volga and Mississippi Rivers—which acted as spring boards for the great drive into the frontier regions. The Russian pioneers (Cossacks) were lured to the frontier by furs, silver, and trading opportunities with primitive peoples. They built forts, fought natives, and were followed into the frontier by organized emigrations which were in turn followed by the promoters. The parallels to nineteenth-century America are quite evident.

The American frontier movement provides striking similarities with the frontier movement in Australia, and especially the one in Canada. One historian, A. L. Burt, suggests that:

> If Frederick Jackson Turner had looked North when he wrote about the American West, he might have discovered a surprising confirmation of (his) thesis . . .[4]

It is important to recognize that frontier movements are universal and not solely confined to the history of America. The attention of this volume, however, will be focused directly upon the American frontier movement. Although the westward movement had neither a precise beginning nor an abrupt ending, it was of paramount importance from the middle of the eighteenth century to the 1890's. These have been described as the formative years in American history.

Did the process of filling a primitive and empty continent leave an imprint? There are those who minimize the effects, and there are those who contend that the frontier imprint on American society is indelible. This is one of the major problems with which the subsequent chapters will grapple.

[4] Reprinted with permission of the copyright owners, The Regents of the University of Wisconsin, from Walker D. Wayman and Clifton B. Kroeber, eds., *The Frontier in Perspective*, p. 60, 1957, The University of Wisconsin Press.

1 | The Frontier Hypothesis

Frederick Jackson Turner is regarded as one of America's greatest and most influential historians. Writing during the last decade of the nineteenth century and the early years of the twentieth century, the young historian from Wisconsin developed and advanced a new interpretation of American history which has become known as the "frontier hypothesis" or the Turner thesis. Turner has ceased to be the *last* word in frontier history, but it is most appropriate that he have the *first* word in a study concerned with the Western experience.

Turner was born during the early months of the Civil War, November 14, 1861, in Portage, Wisconsin—a small frontier community. Turner commented on his birthplace while delivering a lecture to the students of the Harvard History Club in 1923.

> My Birthplace was at the portage where Father Marquette crossed from the Fox to the Wisconsin on his journey down the Mississippi, and which was the highway of many another explorer, but I am forced to admit that this made no impression upon my mind.[1]

Young Turner was impressed, however, with the European elements in the town of Portage. He described the village as a "frontier melting-pot" where one frequently encountered a wide range of immigrants including German merchants, Scottish farmers, Irish raftsmen of the river, and numerous settlements of Norwegians, English and Swiss. The curious thing to Turner was the manner in which these people of divergent cultural and national backgrounds were capable of merging together into a single community.

The historian's father, Andrew Jackson Turner, migrated from Plattsburg, New York, to Portage, where he became a journalist, Republican politician and local historian. Existing evidence reveals that A. J. Turner was warmly admired by his son and therefore had a strong influence on the boy— always commending the virtues of initiative, self-reliance and hard work. Fritz was given the best education the state had to offer, yet, he stated in later years that his real education came from his father's newspaper office where he worked as a typesetter. There he gained a firsthand knowledge of life in Portage and especially frontier politics.

In 1884, Turner received his B.A. degree from the University of Wisconsin and for a brief time was a reporter on Chicago and Milwaukee newspapers. Dissatisfied with his work, Turner decided to return to the university and prepare for a career in history. He completed the requirements for

[1] Jacobs, ed., *F. J. Turner's Legacy: Unpublished Writings in American History,* pp. 4–5.

his M.A. degree in 1888 and immediately enrolled at Johns Hopkins University for his doctoral work. In 1890, he was awarded the Ph.D. degree for his dissertation, "The Character and Influence of the Indian Trade in Wisconsin."

It was during these years of work on his advanced degrees that Turner came into contact with the influences that contributed so heavily to the development of his surprisingly modern views of history. At the University of Wisconsin he was fortunate in having the opportunity to study with some remarkable professors such as the renowned historian William F. Allen. Professor Allen was teaching the new and radical view that society was an evolving organism—an idea which had an unusually strong impact on Turner and became the foundation of his later historical concepts regarding the American frontier.

While pursuing his studies at Johns Hopkins, Turner's concepts were further molded by the teachings of Woodrow Wilson, a political scientist, Richard Ely, an economist, and by his principal instructor, Herbert Adams. Professor Adams, a confirmed believer in the "germ theory" of history, contended that the origins of democratic institutions in America could be traced all the way back to "germs" in medieval Europe. Turner found himself nourishing a negative attitude toward this concept. He did not deny the germ theory, but he believed that equal emphasis had to be given to environmental forces which not only altered the original germs, but oftentimes produced mutations. Many years later, Turner remarked of Adams' teaching.

> The frontier [thesis] was pretty much a *reaction* from that due to my indignation.[2]

It was during the early years of his tenure at the University of Wisconsin that Turner gave expression to his famous frontier hypothesis. In the summer of 1893, he was invited to present a paper at a special meeting of the American

[2] Billington, *Frontier and Section,* p. 3.

Historical Association held at the World's Columbian Exposition in Chicago. Under the title, "The Significance of the Frontier in American History," Turner presented a fresh and meaningful approach to the understanding of American history. At first the essay attracted very little attention, but time soon brought recognition, and it became a monumental landmark in American historical writing.

The most accurate way to explain the frontier thesis is to allow Turner to speak for himself. The following quotations are selected from his famous 1893 essay.

[Definition of the Frontier]

Up to our own day American history has been in a large degree the history of the colonization of the Great West. The existence of an area of free land, its continuous recession, and the advance of American settlement westward, explain American development . . . . The peculiarity of American institutions is, the fact that they have been compelled to adapt themselves to the changes of an expanding people—to the changes involved in crossing a continent, in winning a wilderness . . . . American development has exhibited not merely advance along a single line, but a return to primitive conditions on a continually advancing frontier line, and a new development for that area. American social development has been continually beginning over again on the frontier . . . . In this advance, the frontier is the outer edge of the wave—the meeting point between savagery and civilization. The most significant thing about the American frontier is, that it lies at the hither edge of free land. In the census reports it is treated as the margin of that settlement which has a density of two or more to the square mile. The term is an elastic one, and for our purpose does not need sharp definition . . . . This paper will make no attempt to treat the subject exhaustively; its aim

is simply to call attention to the frontier as a
fertile field for investigation, and to suggest some
of the problems which arise in connection with
it . . . .

[The Power of the American Environment]

In the settlement of America we have to observe
how European life entered the continent, and how
America modified and developed that life and re-
acted on Europe. Our early history is the study of
European germs developing in an American environment . . . . The wilderness masters the colonist. It finds him a European in dress, industries,
tools, modes of travel, and thought. It takes him
from the railroad car and puts him in the birch
canoe. It strips off the garments of civilization and
arrays him in the hunting shirt and the moccasin.
It puts him in the log cabin . . . . Before long he
has gone to planting Indian corn and plowing with
a sharp stick; . . . In short, at the frontier the
environment is at first too strong for the man.
He must accept the conditions which it furnishes,
or perish, and so . . . . Little by little he transforms
the wilderness, but the outcome is not the old Europe . . . The fact is, that here is a new product
that is American . . . . Moving westward, the
frontier became more and more American . . . .
Thus the advance of the frontier has meant a
steady movement away from the influence of Europe . . . . And to study this advance the men
who grew up under these conditions, and the political, economic, and social results of it, is to
study the really American part of our history . . . .

[The Successive Frontier Waves]

The Atlantic frontier was compounded of fisherman, fur-trader, miner, cattle-raiser, and farmer.
Excepting the fisherman, each type of industry

was on the march toward the West . . . . Each
passed in successive waves across the continent.
Stand at Cumberland Gap and watch the procession of civilization, marching single file—the
buffalo following the trail to the salt springs,
the Indian, the fur-trader and hunter, the cattle-
raiser, the pioneer farmer—and the frontier passed
by. Stand at South Pass in the Rockies a century
later and see the same procession with wider intervals between. The unequal rate of advance com-
pels us to distinguish the frontier into the trader's
frontier, the rancher's frontier, or the miner's frontier, and the farmer's frontier. When the mines
and the cow pens were still near the fall line the
traders' pack trains were trickling across the Alle-
ghanies . . . . When the trappers scaled the Rockies,
the farmer was still near the mouth of the Missouri.

[Effects of the Frontier on American Government]

First, we note that the frontier promoted the formation of a composite nationality for the American
people . . . . In another way the advance of the
frontier decreased our dependence on England
. . . . The legislation which most developed the
powers of the national government, and played
the largest part in its activity, was conditioned
on the frontier . . . . The growth of nationalism
and the evolution of American political institutions were dependent on the advance of the frontier . . . . The pioneer needed goods of the coast,
and so the grand series of internal improvement
and railroad legislation began, with potent nation-
alizing effects . . . . Loose construction increased as
the nation marched westward . . . . The purchase
of Louisiana was perhaps the constitutional turning point in the history of the Republic, inasmuch
as it afforded both a new area for national legislation and the occasion of the downfall of the policy

of strict construction. But the purchase of Louisiana was called out by frontier needs and demands. As frontier states accrued to the Union the national power grew . . . . In 1789 the States were the creators of the Federal Government; in 1861 the Federal Government was the creator of a large majority of the States . . . . the most important effect of the frontier has been in the promotion of democracy . . . . the frontier is productive of individualism. Complex society is [diluted] by the wilderness into a kind of primitive organization based on the family . . . .

[Effects of the Frontier on American Character]

From the conditions of frontier life came intellectual traits of profound importance . . . . That coarseness and strength combined with acuteness and inquisitiveness; that practical, inventive turn of mind, quick to find expedients; that masterful grasp of material things, lacking in the artistic but powerful to effect great ends; that restless, nervous energy; that dominant individualism, working for good and for evil, and withal that buoyancy and exuberance which comes with freedom—those are traits of the frontier, or traits called out elsewhere because of the existence of the frontier . . . the people of the United States have taken their tone from the incessant expansion . . . . Movement has been its dominant fact . . . . The stubborn American environment is there with its imperious summons to accept its conditions; the inherited ways of doing things are also there; and yet, in spite of environment, and in spite of custom, each frontier did indeed furnish a new field of opportunity, a gate of escape from the bondage of the past; and freshness, and confidence, and scorn of older society, impatience of its restraints and its ideas, and indifference to its lessons, have accompanied the frontier.

[Conclusion]

> And now, four centuries from the discovery of
> America, at the end of a hundred years of life
> under the Constitution, the frontier has gone, and
> with its going has closed the first period of Ameri-
> can history.[3]

Though he was only thirty-two years old and just recently
at work in his teaching career, Frederick Jackson Turner
presented a thesis which revolutionized social studies and has
become one of the most widely known essays in American
history. During the three decades following the delivery of
his address, the entire framework of American historical
writing and teaching was altered. For a whole generation
American historians studied the development of the United
States in relationship to the frontier process.

The new urban-industrial society of the 1890's had already
reached the stage of nostalgia for a vanished frontier, and its
myths were treasured as a national heritage. The dime novel
with a Western theme had created an exciting stereotype of
the West. Consequently, Turner's essay captured the imagination of the reading public as well as the historical profession.

To the theme of his early address, "The Significance of the
Frontier in American History," Turner referred again and
again in his later writings and speeches. On each of these
occasions, Turner either added clarification to or expanded
his original thesis. In 1896, while giving a dedication address,
he added a new dimension to his thesis by describing the
frontier as a "safety valve."

> Americans had a safety valve for social danger, a
> bank account on which they might continually
> draw to meet losses. This was the vast unoccupied
> domain that stretched from the borders of the
> settled area to the Pacific Ocean . . . . No grave so-
> cial problem could exist while the wilderness at

[3] *Ibid.*, pp. 37–62.

14

the edge of civilizations opened wide its portals
to all who were oppressed . . . .

Another of Turner's major arguments regarding the frontier was that it developed a distinctive style of American
democracy. He gave this argument a very clear expression in
an address given at the University of Washington in 1914.

American democracy was born of no theorist's
dream; it was not carried in the *Sarah Constant*
to Virginia, nor in the *Mayflower* to Plymouth.
It came out of the American forest, and it gained
new strength each time it touched a new frontier.
Not the constitution, but free land and an abundance of natural resources open to a fit people,
made the democratic type of society in America
for three centuries . . . .[4]

Even after his retirement, Turner continued to comment
on the character of his thesis. In a letter to a friend during
the late 1920's, he wrote:

As you know, the "West" with which I dealt, was
a *process* rather than a fixed geographical region:
it emphasized the way in which the East colonized
the West, and how the "West", as it stood at any
given period affected the development and ideas
of the older areas to the East . . . .[5]

As the years passed, Turner became aware that he was
being increasingly identified as the "Western" or "frontier"
historian. He disliked being labeled because he felt it over-
simplified and distorted his true concepts. Never did Turner
claim that his frontier theory was the only key to the interpretation of American history. On the contrary, he repeatedly

[4] Billington, *op. cit.,* pp. 100–101.
[5] Jacobs, "Frederick Jackson Turner," *The American West* Magazine,
Vol. I, 1964, p. 32.

emphasized Multiple Causation in history. To Turner, there was not a single key or simple explanation of human behavior—either in terms of economics, politics, sociology or even the frontier. All were interwoven as motivating forces and each force had to be thoroughly investigated and its interrelationship with all other forces exactly understood. While writing to a former student, Carl Becker, in 1925, Turner pointed out how his treatment of the frontier had been misinterpreted.

> Although my work has laid stress upon two aspects of American history—the frontier and the sections—I do not think of myself as primarily . . . . a western historian . . . . I have stressed these two factors, because it seemed to me that they had been neglected, but fundamentally I have been interested in the interrelations of economics, politics, sociology, culture in general, with the geographic factors, in explaining the United States of today by means of its history thus broadly taken.[6]

Earlier in 1922, while introducing a lecture on sectionalism to his students, Turner revealed his impatience with the divisions in the social sciences.

> Whether to call this lecture a historical, geographical, political, economic or sociological discussion, I do not know, and I don't much care, for I am one of those who believes in breaking line fences, even at the risk of arrest for trespass, or disclosure of being an amateur, or something worse, breaking into the professional's game.[7]

To suggest that Turner explained American history solely in terms of the frontier is to distort the truth and discredit the man's true breadth of understanding. In the early 1920's, Turner prepared a companion essay to the one he delivered in 1893. In this second essay, entitled "The Significance of

[6] *Ibid.* p. 34.
[7] Jacobs, *F. J. Turner's Legacy,* p. 47.

Sections in American History," he gave his finest analysis of the interrelationship of forces.

> No single factor is determinative. Men are not absolutely dictated to by climate, geography, soils, or economic interests. The influence of the stock from which they sprang, the inherited ideals, the spiritual factors, often triumph over the material interests. There is also the influence of personality.[8]

Reputation and opportunity continued to increase for Turner. During the late 1890's, he received a steady flow of offers to teach at such leading universities as Princeton, Amherst, the University of Chicago, Johns Hopkins, Stanford and the University of California. The pressure of these offers forced the Wisconsin regents to lessen his teaching load. By 1906, his only book published during his lifetime, *The Rise of the New West: 1814–1829,* made its debut. In 1909, Turner became President of the American Historical Association, and the following year he accepted a teaching position at Harvard University.

As a teacher, Turner was very successful. He radiated an extraordinary personal influence over his students, always giving a keen interest to their work. Students flocked to his seminars, which they affectionately referred to as the "Wild West Show." Turner maintained his sense of humor, however, and did not misinterpret these occasional ribbings. His approach to teaching the West was neither dramatic nor romantic, but instead, intellectual and scholarly.

Turner's interest in his students was not confined to the work they did in his classroom. He always found time to give them advice and criticism. To one of his students, who had just entered the teaching profession, Turner wrote the following words of encouragement:

[8] Turner, "Sections and Nation," *The Yale Review* (Copyright Yale University Press), XII, Oct. 1922, pp. 1–21.

> I have taught general history and medieval history,
> and English history, and recent modern history,
> and elocution, and have run a correspondence
> course in Oriental history! So I know some of
> your trials, But such things do broaden the view,
> if you live through them, and better men than
> either of us have been all the better for having
> occupied a settee instead of a chair. Cheer up,
> and take Dr. Walter Camp's Daily Dozen Exer-
> cises (price 10 cents).[9]

Turner taught at Harvard from 1910 until his retirement
in 1924. Following his retirement he became a research asso-
ciate at the Huntington Library in 1927 and remained in
that position until his death, March 14, 1932.

In the final analysis, Turner was concerned with every
aspect of civilization. He was as much interested in literature,
arts, immigration and industrialization as he was in the West.
Because of his unusually wide range of interest and research,
he understood the history of America better than most historians of his generation. It is highly significant that shortly
before his death, he outlined a new essay to match his previous essays on the frontier and the section. The title of the
work was, "The Significance of the City in American Civilization."

The Turner Critics

The Turner thesis remained almost unchallenged until the
1920's. But during that decade a whole procession of scholars
began to issue savage attacks upon the frontier thesis which
soon took the form of an anti-Turnerian revolt. Throughout
the next twenty years, the bulk of scholarly opinion ran
heavily against the Turner thesis.

Although the critics held great respect for Dr. Turner, they

[9] Jacobs, "Frederick Jackson Turner," *Turner, Bolton, and Webb:
Three Historians of the American Frontier*, p. 30.

felt justified in drawing certain critical conclusions about his thesis. Some of them directed their attacks against "contradictions" within the thesis. One of Turner's own disciples remarked:

> He traced the spread of human slavery from old to new regions, there to become more fixed in a stratified western society, and still talked of a growing democracy. He pointed out the hostility of western men to governmental interference and then told of the tendency among frontiersmen on the plains and in the semiarid regions to call on the central government to do things for them which did violence to all laissez faire attitudes. He emphasized the barn-raising, the husking bee, the logrolling, and the neighborhood roundup as normal cooperative efforts among those he depicted as extreme individualists. Everywhere there is contradictions. . . .[10]

After considering a number of frontier traits such as the spread of slavery, the hacienda system, lawlessness, vigilante law, trial without jury and urban racial intolerance—many of the critics questioned Turner's suggestion that the frontier was productive of democracy. Others condemned Turner for his omission or neglect of certain forces in American Western history such as the influence of the Spanish in the Southwest. Finally there are the critics who contend that Turner's thesis contributed a disservice to the nation by turning the country's attention inward just when it needed to be expanding its attention on a world scale.

At this point, it seems highly appropriate that the views of the Turner critics should be heard. The following selected quotations are representative of the major criticisms. As with Turner, each critic will speak for himself.

[10] Hutchinson, William T., ed., *Marcus W. Jernegan Essays in American Historiography*, "Frederick Jackson Turner," by Avery Craven, Russell and Russell, New York, N.Y., 1958.

Louis M. Hacker

Turner and his followers were the fabricators of a tradition which is not only fictitious but also to a very large extent positively harmful . . . . What is of greater concern is the perverted reading Turner gave to American history in his insistence upon the uniqueness of American experience and his emphasis upon sectional development as a sort of flywheel to balance all political, social and economic disparities. The unhappy results, for forty years, were the following: a turning inward of American historical activity at exactly the time when all trained eyes should have been on events going on beyond the country's physical borders; an accumulation of supposed evidences of the development of American institutions entirely in nativistic terms without an understanding of how closely American institutional growth paralleled the European; an almost complete disregard of the basic class antagonisms in American history; and a profound ignorance of the steps by which monopolistic capitalism and imperialism were being developed in the country . . . . Had Turner not so boldly cut himself loose from the currents of European thought . . . had he given more attention to the activities of some of his contemporaries instead of to the Wisconsin fur trade . . . . then our own past, in the light of America's current needs, might not be the sealed book it is today . . . . Only by a study of the origins and growth of American capitalism and imperialism can we obtain insight into the nature and complexity of the problems confronting us today. And I am prepared to submit that perhaps the chief reason for the absence of this proper understanding was the futile hunt for a unique "American spirit" which Frederick Jackson Turner began forty years ago and in which he involved most of America's historical scholars from that time until now.[11]

George Wilson Pierson

Turner stated and restated many times a conviction that . . . . Old World germs were not the really significant factors in our national evolution . . . they were merely the roots, the remote background, the undistinguished platform from which a new departure could be taken . . . a few queries may legitimately be raised at this point . . . it would appear that the woman suffrage idea originated in Europe and found but slim support in the Ohio Valley. The direct dependence of our belated Civil Service legislation on the earlier English movement will be apparent to anyone who cares to investigate that subject. As for manhood suffrage, whatever may have been the contributions of the wilderness frontier, is it not hard to believe that the American democrat sprang, as it were, full-armed, ballot in hand, out of the Western woods? Surely one cannot today dismiss the long evolution of Parliament, the history of Colonial legislatures, the methods of the New England town meeting, the self-government of Congregational churches, and the voting habits of trading-Company stockholders without a thought. This leads to another disconcerting observation. Turner nowhere seriously credits Anglo-American Protestantism with democratic tendencies. One is left to infer that such equalitarian and humanitarian interests as American Christianity has displayed must have derived from the experience of conquering the West . . . . Turner himself did make a number of flat-footed and dogmatic statements, did put forward some highly questionable interpretations, did on occasion guess and not

[11] Hacker, "Sections or Classes," *The Nation,* July 26, 1933, p. 187.

verify, did exaggerate—and stick for more than twenty years to the exaggerations . . . . Did Turner, perhaps on the other hand, put his effort into theory and philosophy, into developing and revising his first grand vision and interpretation? Once again, curiously, our examination indicates that he did not. For not only did he republish his first essay without substantial alteration, but his later essays show little if any advance beyond the position taken in his first. Not only is there small proof of fresh research; there is as little proof of fresh thinking. Elaboration, progress in application, repetition, certainly, but distressingly little in the way of genuine reconsideration or modification. If anything, the later essays are more general, sweeping, and blurred . . . one of the most striking weaknesses of the essays as a whole is internal inconsistency . . . the frontier theory in its full development does not hang together. The nationalism of the frontier does violence to its sectional tendencies, innovations are derived from repetition, the improvement of civilization is achieved via the abandonment of civilization, and materialism gives birth to idealism . . . . In what it proposes, the frontier hypothesis needs painstaking revision. By what it fails to mention, the theory today disqualifies itself as an adequate guide to American development.[12]

Benjamin F. Wright Jr.

In their choice of political institutions the men of this section (Middle-West) were imitative not creative. They were not interested in making experiments. Their constitutional, like their domestic, architecture was patterned after that of the communities from which they had moved westward . . . . It will be remembered that in his original essay on the influence of the frontier Turner wrote

[12] Pierson, "The Frontier and American Institutions," *New England Quarterly,* No. 15, June, 1942.

in the crusading mood of one who battles for a dear and a long neglected cause. It was with vigor and enthusiasm that "he hitched his star to a covered wagon."

. . . The conception of the "transforming influence" of the frontier, as it appears in Turner's essays, is largely a myth. Indeed, I believe that a much better argument can be made out that the hardships of pioneer living transformed a large proportion of the restless and discontented who migrated to the free and promised land into men ambitious to be prosperous citizens in the image of the bankers and merchants and landowners back home . . . . Furthermore it (Frontier Thesis) is in good part a Middle West-sectional interpretation . . . . One has but to compare the differences between the institutions of the English and those of the French, Dutch and Spanish colonies in America to see that the foundations, and more, of our democracy were brought in the *Susan Constant* and *Mayflower*. That democracy did not come out of the American forest unless it was first carried there. On some frontiers democracy was not strengthened, rather the reverse. Free land gave the opportunity to establish slavery in Louisiana, oligarchy in the Mormon state, the hacienda system in Mexican California, while it was furnishing the opportunity for a "fit" people in the Middle West to establish the particular degree and kind of democracy that they favored.[13]

Conclusion

Theories of past historical development are designed to help understand society of today. Therefore, the controversy over the Turner thesis is very important.

[13] Wright, Benjamin, "Political Institutions and the Frontier," in *Sources of Culture in the Middle West,* Dixon Ryan Fox, ed. Appleton-Century-Crofts, New York, 1934.

Frederick Jackson Turner interpreted the Frontier as a process of Americanization in which the force of environment forged a variety of character traits in the American personality. Most of his critics interpreted the frontier as a geographic area which slowly became Europeanized as civilization gradually overcame the hostile environment.

Several pertinent questions emerge from the controversy. Did the West originate new ideas or did it imitate old ones? Did the West assist in the development of democracy or hinder its growth? and finally, disregarding both Turner and his critics, did the whole frontier experience leave any imprint at all on the American character?

Subsequent chapters detail the frontier experience from the 1840's to the 1890's. These chapters are designed to provide information to the reader which will assist him in finding answers to the preceding questions as well as discovering his own reactions to the frontier thesis and its critics.

Bibliography

Babcock, C. Merton	*The American Frontier* Holt, Rinehart, Winston, New York, N.Y.	1965 ed.
Billington, Ray Allen	*America's Frontier Heritage* Holt, Rinehart, Winston, New York, N.Y.	1966 ed.
Billington, Ray Allen	*Frontier and Section* Prentice-Hall, Englewood Cliffs, N.J.	1961 ed.
Billington, Ray Allen	*Westward Expansion* Macmillan, New York, N.Y.	1960 ed.
Clark, Thomas	*Frontier America* Scribner's, New York, N.Y.	1959 ed.
Jacobs, Wilbur, ed.	*Frederick Jackson Turner's Legacy* Huntington Library, San Marino, Calif.	1966 ed.
Jacobs, Caughey, Frantz	*Turner, Bolton and Webb* University of Washington Press, Seattle, Wash.	1965 ed.
Noble, David	*Historians against History* University of Minnesota Press, Minneapolis, Minnesota	1965 ed.

Potter, David	*People of Plenty* University of Chicago Press, Chicago, Ill.	1954 ed.
Richmond-Mardock	*A Nation Moving West* University of Nebraska Press, Lincoln, Neb.	1966 ed.
Riegel-Athearn	*America Moves West* Holt, Rinehart, New York, N.Y.	1964 ed.
Taylor, George	*The Turner Thesis* D. C. Heath, Boston, Mass.	1956 ed.
Wish, Harvey	*The American Historian* Oxford University Press, New York, N.Y.	1960 ed.
Wyman-Kroeber	*The Frontier in Perspective* University of Wisconsin Press, Madison, Wis.	1965 ed.

Periodicals

Hacker, Louis	"Sections or Classes," *The Nation*	July 26, 1933
Jacobs, Wilbur	"Frederick Jackson Turner," *The American West*, Vol. I, number 1, Palo Alto, Calif.	1964

Address

Johansen, Dorothy	"A Working Hypothesis for the Study of Migrations," the Ameri- can Historical Association	1966

2 | The Warriors

According to Turner the effect of the Indian frontier was important as a consolidating agent in our history, and that from the close of the seventeenth century various inter-colonial congresses had been called to treaty with the Indians and establish common measures of defense. The Indian was a common danger that demanded united action on the part of the colonists. Turner saw the frontier as a military training school which kept alive the power of resistance to aggression, and developed the stalwart and rugged qualities of the frontiersman. Some credit for the development of these rugged qualities in the frontiersmen is due the American Indian.

The American Indian served as a brake on the headlong rush to settle the frontier, to plunder the land, and to destroy its natural resources. While slowing the rapid pace of frontier settlement, the Indian provided time for thoughtful Americans of the late nineteenth century time to develop a policy of conservation and protection of the nation's resources.

Indian Heritage

America's heritage has been enriched by the contributions of the Indian. Hundreds of geographic place names from Manhattan to Seattle are of Indian origin as are the names of nearly half our states. The appreciation of nature as expressed in the Indians' stories, music, dances, and painting are now being recognized by other Americans and these talents are being encouraged. The architecture of the Pueblo Indians has become popular in the Southwest. Tobacco, which was one of over fifty crops and food plants introduced by the Indians, permitted the economic survival of Virginia during the Colonial period. The Indian game of lacrosse has provided Canada with one of its most popular games. American literature, the impact of Indian lore, is reflected in James Fenimore Cooper's novel, *The Last of the Mohicans,* which is one of the best known American novels. *Laughing Boy,* by Oliver La Farge, won the Pulitzer Prize for its portrayal of a Navajo's difficulties in resolving the conflicts between his society and that of other Americans.

At the time of America's discovery, there were perhaps no more than one million Indians in North America. But these comparatively few Indians, by modern population standards, outnumbered the European explorers and colonizers for nearly two centuries. Europeans were confused by the many differing customs and languages of the Indians with whom they came in contact—a situation very dissimilar to the relatively well-defined customs and languages in Europe. Poor relationships between Indians and Europeans were caused by misunderstandings of Indian customs on the part of the Europeans. One commonly held misconception was

27

that all Indians were hunters, too primitive to engage in agriculture or to develop any system of property. Wherever soil, moisture, and growing seasons permitted, the native inhabitants of North America planted tobacco, corn, squash, and beans. Stores of Indian corn helped the settlers at Plymouth survive that first winter of 1620.

The Spanish colonial policy aimed at conquering the Indians, many of whom were sedentary farmers in our Southwest, Christianizing them if possible, and then making the Indians useful Spanish subjects. French interest in the fur trade dictated another policy with the Indians, one of friendship. The fur trade was mutually advantageous to *voyageurs* and Indians alike. The French intermingled with the Indian, while the English settlers cleared the forests and destroyed the game, driving the Indians from their hunting grounds.

Historians speculate that the first migrations of Indians from Asia to North America occurred nearly 35,000 years ago. In a study of the American frontier, the study of the Indian must of necessity be limited to a relatively short span of time. The two following quotations encompass this time, and offer a contrast.

> Whereas it is just and reasonable . . . that the several nations or tribes of Indians with whom we are connected, and who live under our protection, should not be molested or disturbed in the possession of such parts of our dominions and territories as, not having been ceded to or purchased by us, are reserved to them . . . as their hunting grounds.[1]

> I am tired of fighting . . . My people ask me for food, and I have none to give. It is cold, and we have no blankets, no wood. My people are starving to death. Where is my little daughter? I do not

[1] From *Documents of American History* (7th Ed.) p. 48. (© 1963 by Meredith Publishing Co. Reprinted by permission of Appleton-Century-Crofts, New York, N.Y.)

know. Perhaps, even now, she is freezing to death.
Hear me, my chiefs. I have fought; but from
where the sun now stands, Joseph will fight no
more forever.[2]

Little more than one hundred years elapsed between the
issuance of the first statement, from the Proclamation of
1763, and the utterance of the second statement by Chief
Joseph of the Nez Percé at the time of his surrender to United
States troops in 1877. During the intervening century, the
way of life of the American Indian was drastically changed
from that of a warrior-hunter to that of a ward of the United
States government.

Mutual hostility and mistrust existed between the Indian
and the white man. The Proclamation of 1763 was intended
to ease the difficulties between white settlers and Indians of
the Old Northwest by preventing further expansion of the
colonists beyond the Appalachian Mountains. The Indian
territorial boundaries established by the first agreement were
soon pushed back; and so, too, were the boundaries of the
last Indian Territory eliminated approximately one hundred
twenty-five years later.

James Fenimore Cooper's novels helped to stereotype the
American Indian as the skilled hunter and brave warrior of
the eastern forests. As our knowledge of the Indian becomes
more extensive, we realize that he was not a stereotype—that
in reality, many differences existed among numerous Indian
cultures. As there were many Indian cultures, so too, there
were over a dozen major language groups and over two hundred different tribes in North America.

To study something about each of these groups of Indians
would be confusing and would leave us with very little understanding of any one of them. In our study of the Indian
frontier, we shall select the Teton-Dakota of the Sioux tribe
as being the most representative of the kind of Indians en-

[2] *American Heritage Book of Indians,* p. 316. (Courtesy, American
Heritage Publishing Co., Inc.)

countered by the settlers of the last frontier, the northern Great Plains.

The Sioux

What is the most typical Indian culture? Is it that of the eastern forest Indians, or of the Indians of the Western mountains, or that of the Indians of the Great Plains? Robert H. Lowie has stated:

> Most of us, when we think of Indians, envision such items as tipis, war bonnets with trailing feathers, Sitting Bull, ponies, and buffaloes. In other words, we have all come to think of the Plains Indians as the genuine Indian, the ideal Indian—the very quintessence of Indian-ness. In many ways, however, the Plains Indians were a highly distinctive group and lived in a rather specialized way or at least in a manner quite different from other kinds of Indians. They were no more typical of the American Indian than the Navajo, the Hopi, or the Iroquois. Yet through the accidents of history, perhaps also by their own role, often heroic, in the epic of the West or indeed as the result of the insistent stereotype of the movies, they have come to usurp in the public mind all other Indians and to represent *the* Indian way of life.[3]

Walter Prescott Webb, an authority on the Great Plains, explains why the Indians of the Great Plains have come to symbolize the typical American Indian:

> The Plains Indians constituted for a much longer time than we realize the most effectual barrier

[3] From *Indians of the Plains* (p. ix) by Robert H. Lowie. (© 1954 by the American Museum of Natural History. By permission of Doubleday and Co.)

30

ever set up by a native American population against European invaders in a temperate zone. For two and a half centuries they maintained themselves with great fortitude against the Spanish, English, French, Mexican, Texan, and American invaders, withstanding missionaries, whisky, disease, gunpowder, and lead.[4]

Asked to name one group of Plains Indians, most Americans would not hesitate long before they answered by naming the Sioux. In introducing his study of the great warrior society, Royal Hassrick stated:

For many people the Sioux, as warriors and as buffalo hunters, have become the symbol of all that is Indian—colorful figures endowed with great fortitude and powerful vision. They were the heroes of the Great Plains in the day of heroes and they were the villains, too.[5]

The Siouan language family included many tribes of north-central United States. The most powerful of the Sioux family were the Dakota—the Santee-Dakota east of the Missouri River, and the Teton-Dakota west of the Missouri. The French fur trappers first noted the Sioux as being woodland Indians living in the region of the upper Minnesota River in the 1600's; but by 1800, the Teton-Dakota had migrated west, acquired the horse and became typical Plains Indians. In migrating west of the Missouri River, the Teton-Dakota split into many tribes: Brulés, Oglalas, Miniconjous, Sans Arcs, Two Kettles, Hunkpapas, and Blackfoot. These tribes claimed as their hunting lands, the plains of western South Dakota in the early 1800's. The area hunted by the Teton-Dakota was, however, but a part of the Great Plains which

[4] *Great Plains,* p. 48. (By Permission of Blaisdell Publishing Co., Division of Ginn & Co.)
[5] From *The Sioux* (p. ix) by Royal B. Hassrick (© 1964 by permission of the University of Oklahoma Press.)

cover a vast area from the Missouri River on the east to the Rocky Mountains on the west. And from the Rio Grande in the south, these level, treeless, and semi-arid grasslands extend north into Canada.

Contrary to popular belief, most Indians were not good conservationists, and the Teton-Dakota were no exception. It was the custom, in the fall of the year, to burn off the dry grass in order to insure an early growth of new grass in the spring; but these prairie fires also destroyed timber along the rivers as well as animal life. So wasteful of the resources were Sioux of South Dakota, that many were forced to move west into the high plains of Wyoming by the winter of the "Big Issue," the first treaty at Fort Laramie, 1851. It was in this Great Plains region, east and west of the Black Hills, that the old nomadic way of life of these great Sioux warrior—the Teton-Dakota—came to an end.

The Massacre of Wounded Knee marked the final defeat of the Sioux, and it occurred in the year 1890—the same year in which the Bureau of the Census announced that the American frontier was officially closed. Since the end of the Civil War, the Sioux had opposed incursions upon their Powder River Country by emigrants bound for Oregon, by cattlemen establishing cattle trails to Montana, and by railroad builders who were surveying the northern limits of the hunting grounds guaranteed the Indians by the second treaty of Fort Laramie.

The culture of the Indians of the Great Plains, and particularly the culture of the Sioux, was among the last to give way to the white man's reservation. Professor Walter Webb lists the following facts of the culture of the Plains Indians:

1. They were nomadic, they were not farmers.
2. Often called "The buffalo Indians", they depended upon the great herds of these animals to supply all their necessities.
3. Their weapons were adapted to the hunting of big game, the buffalo.

4. Theirs was a "horse culture." This animal revolutionized their way of life long before the coming of white civilization.[6]

The Indians of the high Plains had no permanent homes, though they retained favorite hunting and camping areas. They moved about constantly in search of food—their food being primarily the buffalo. This continual movement in following the buffalo affected nearly every aspect of their existence.

The term *tipi* is Dakota in its origin, and this conical tent of nomadic American Indians was well adapted to a people always on the move. The foundation of a Teton-Dakota tipi was three poles with some twenty additional poles used as supports. The Teton-Dakota used more poles in their tipis than most Plains Indians because of the availability of timber in the Black Hills and Bighorn Mountains. Ten to twelve buffalo hides sewn together served as the cover of a tipi. The foundation poles were laid on the ground and tied together near one end and raised. The supporting poles were then tied to the foundation poles. The buffalo-hide cover was raised by the last pole and pulled around the tipi until it met in front. The overlapping cover was held together by wooden pegs. The cover was pulled taut by moving the supporting poles tightly against it. The two gaps on either side of the smoke hole could be adjusted by movement of the two outside poles to which they were attached. A tipi could be fifteen to eighteen feet high and approximately fifteen feet in diameter.

The tipi covering was decorated with porcupine quill trimming (beads often replaced quills after the coming of white traders) and painted with various symbols, which Professor of Anthropology, Ruth Underhill, states commonly fell in one of three classes: the mythical originator and his wife, their home, or their trails. A skin curtain shielded the narrow opening in the cover of the tipi, this entrance usually faced east and the place of honor was opposite the entrance.

[6] Webb, *op. cit.*, p. 52.

All the work of erecting the tipi, or of taking it down, was performed by the women. A tipi could be taken down, packed, and with its furnishings, loaded on a travois in fifteen minutes. Two Indian women could raise a tipi and set up a household in about an hour's time. The portability of the tipi made it especially suited to a nomadic people. The shape of the tipi provided warm living quarters in the cold winters of the Great Plains by reducing the amount of heat required to warm the lower portions. During the hot summer days, the sides of the tipi could be rolled up to provide more ventilation.

The moving of camp was a coordinated and disciplined undertaking. The decision to move was made by the Nacas who were the civil authorities of the tribe. Certain ones of the soldier societies were selected to lead the procession. Their duties also included keeping the people in order and preventing members of the tribe from wandering off to hunt. Punishment was administered to those who intentionally disobeyed these "police." When a good camping site was chosen—one which provided a good supply of water, grazing for the horses, and some protection from enemies—the families would begin erecting tipis. The village followed no particular pattern as to the placement of tipis; relatives often placed their tipis near one another.

With the availability of food in the summer, camps tended to be larger than in the winter when food sources were limited and the increased need for firewood dictated somewhat smaller villages. Particularly severe winters brought starvation and the necessity for individual hunters to set out in search of food. Winter was the time for the making of tools and bows and arrows. Although the changes in seasons did not greatly affect the activities of the Plains Indians, certain seasonal occurrences did influence them, as observed in the names by which they recognized the various "moons" which would roughly correspond with our months.

December was referred to by some as Moon of Frost in the Tipi; January was the Tree Popping Moon because the extreme cold would cause trees to split with a loud noise; February caused snow blindness and was referred to as Sore Eyes Moon. Activities for the remainder of the year are indicated by such descriptions as March—the Moon when the Grain Comes Up; April—the Moon of the Birth of Calves, saw the Dakota still in their sheltered winter camps. The coming of spring meant increased activity, dances, ceremonial affairs, communal hunts.

Summer was the time of vision-seeking and the sun dance. A young man sought power from some supernatural being or spirit. Without such supernatural aid, he had little hope for success as a warrior or a hunter. The vision quest usually lasted four days, in which time the Indians fasted and thirsted. In some instances, he sought the pity of a spirit by self-mutilation. As a result of this seclusion and privation, the Indian worked himself into such an emotional state that he might experience what to him was a revelation or a vision. In his vision, the subject was befriended by a supernatural being, usually some animal or bird. Thereafter, he might wear a token of this vision or paint it on his shield cover. He might be instructed in the vision as to the sacred objects which should be assembled for his "medicine bundle."

The sun dance was common to nearly all the Plains Indians. Those participating went without food or water. They would fix their gaze upon the top of the sun dance pole—upon which a buffalo skull, or some other symbolic object had been placed—rising up and down on their toes, or shuffling backward and forward. They sought to bring about a vision which might give them power, or remove some worry or problem. A Dakota would participate in a sun dance in fulfillment of a vow made to the supernaturals, while seeking their help in a difficult situation. In this ceremony, the Dakota was known to use self-torture. The torture consisted of running skewers through the muscles of the chest or back, attaching the skewers to the sun dance pole with thongs, and pulling from the thongs until the skewers were torn through the flesh.

Fall was the busiest time of year for the Plains Indians. Hunting was most important, for a large food supply had to be laid up for the winter. Women cut up the meat and dried it or made pemmican of it by mixing it with dried, crushed berries and stored it in skin bags after adding melted fat and marrow. With the snows of winter, the Indian bands again moved to favorite sheltered camp sites.

The Buffalo Hunt

The Plains Indians were dependent upon the buffalo for their way of life. This fact was fully appreciated by frontiersmen familiar with the Great Plains and Indians such as the Teton-Dakota. One of these old frontiersmen was a buffalo-hunter, or "runner" as hunters were called, Frank H. Mayer who as an old man observed:

> . . . the buffalo served his mission, fulfilled his destiny in the history of the Indian, by furnishing him everything he needed—food, clothing, a home, traditions, even a theology. But the buffalo didn't fit in so well with the white man's encroaching civilization . . . the buffalo was hunted and killed with the connivance, yes, the cooperation, of the Government itself. . . .
>
> Don't understand that any official action was taken in Washington and directives sent out to kill all the buff on the plains. Nothing like that happened. What did happen was that army officers in charge of plains operations encouraged the slaughter of buffalo in every possible way. Part of this encouragement was of a practical nature that we runners appreciated. It consisted of ammunition, free ammunition . . . . All you had to do to get it was apply at any frontier army post . . . .
>
> . . . One afternoon I was visiting this man [a high ranking officer in the plains service] in his quarters. . . . we smoked and talked. He said to me:

> "Mayer, there's no two ways about it: either the buffalo or the Indian must go. Only when the Indian becomes absolutely dependent on us for his every need, will we be able to handle him. He's too independent with the buffalo. But if we kill the buffalo we conquer the Indian. It seems a more humane thing to kill the buffalo than the Indian, so the buffalo must go," he concluded.[7]

When buffalo were near, the Indians lived well. There was more than enough to eat and leisure time to paint tipis, to embroider clothing, moccasins, and parfleches (skin bags) with the glass beads secured from white men eager to trade for buffalo robes. There was time for gambling, horse racing, and storytelling. But when the buffalo were not in their territory, the Indians often went hungry. The Plains Indians were, quite literally, "buffalo Indians."

In addition to their dependency upon the buffalo for meat, the Plains Indians utilized nearly every other part of the animal. Tipi coverings, blankets, shield covers, clothing, moccasins, containers, all were made from buffalo skins, either rawhide or leather. In preparing the hides, they were first staked out on the ground with the hairy side down, and the women would scrape away fat, muscle, and tissue with a bone flesher. The clean hide was bleached in the sun for several days and again scraped to an even thickness. Sometimes the hair was removed from the rawhide. If leather was desired for clothing or soft pouches, the rawhide had to be tanned. A mixture of buffalo fat and brain was rubbed thoroughly into the surface of the rawhide which was dried in the sun, stretched, and rubbed with a stone to make the leather pliable.

Buffalo bones were made into tools such as arrow shaft straighteners, sometimes for arrow heads, and for awls which the women used to punch sinew through hides in sewing them together. Sinew, from the tendons of the buffalo, was

[7] Mayer & Ross, *The Buffalo Harvest,* pp. 27–30.

made into bowstrings and used where strong bindings were necessary. Buffalo horns were worn in headdresses and as ornaments; horn spoons and dishes were also fashioned. Lariats were woven from the hair of the buffalo. Glue was secured from boiled horns and hoofs. The rough side of a buffalo tongue was even made useful—as a hair brush by some of the Plains people.

Within some of the Indian tribes were buffalo clans. All Plains Indians held buffalo dances. The Oglala-Sioux (a tribe of the Teton-Dakota) referred to the country north of the Platte river as the Buffalo North and the country on the other side of the river as the Buffalo South. During the early decades of the 1800's the buffalo may have numbered as many as twenty millions on the Great Plains. Emigrants, hunters, and even the Indians themselves slaughtered the buffalo in such great numbers that by the time the frontier was proclaimed to be at an end, the buffalo was near extinction.

Contributing to the comparative ease with which the buffalo were slaughtered was the nature of the animal itself. The reason buffalo runners were not referred to as hunters was the defenselessness of the animal. The buffalo has been described as "unquestionably the stupidest game animal in the world." His eyesight was extremely poor, his hearing was little better, and even his scent was faulty. All the buffalo could do was run when endangered, but most often the great beast was unaware of the danger posed by a hunter.

The acquisition of the horse by the Plains Indians did not create a nomadic way of life because it had already existed. The horse did, however, allow the Indian to travel greater distances in shorter periods of time. The Indians continued to employ much the same techniques in hunting the buffalo, but with a much greater degree of success in the hunt. Four major forms of collective hunting were practiced by the Plains Indians: the "surround", driving the buffalo over a cliff, impounding the animals, or encircling them with fire. The horse greatly aided the surround method; the mounted

Indians would surround the herd, get the animals to milling around, then shoot them down with bows and arrows. Running buffalo over a cliff's edge was a favorite method of securing large amounts of meat. If the cliff were not high enough to kill the animals, a corral was built at the bottom and the animals who had been stampeded over the cliff and into the corral were then killed. Much the same technique was used in the method of impounding the buffalo. Men and women would be strung out in two converging lines. These two lines would funnel the buffalo into a natural, or a man-made enclosure. The buffalo might be lured into the enclosure by Indians who covered themselves with buffalo robes and imitated the bleat of a buffalo calf, while moving in the direction of the enclosure. Before the use of the horse in hunting, the Indians would often start the buffalo toward the enclosure by firing the grass behind them.

Whatever method was used, the weapons employed had to be capable of bringing down an animal which weighed some eighteen hundred pounds. Bows and arrows, clubs, spears, and shields were the weapons used both in hunting and in warfare. Wood of the ash tree was considered by the Sioux to be best for bow-making. The wood was shaped and dried for about two weeks. Final shaping began at the grip, and the ends of the bow were tapered later. The bow was cut to about the height of the owner's waist and the thickness depended upon his grip. The sinew-backed bow was favored by the Western Indians. These bows had three to five layers of sinew glued to the back of them, and were harder hitting than one-piece bows. Bowstrings were made of sinew, shredded, soaked, and rolled together, interlocking the strands into one string which was three times the length of the bow. The bowstring was then folded into thirds, twisted to form a three-ply bowstring, stretched, dried, and attached to the bow by knotting the bowstring outside the notches on either end of the bow. The bow was made taut by tightening the knot at the end, but a bow was never left taut except when in use.

In the time it would take a white man, armed with a cap and ball rifle, to fire and reload, an Indian could discharge up to twenty arrows and ride three hundred yards. Little wonder that the Colt revolver found ready acceptance in the West after its invention in the late 1830's. Indian men were taught early how to make weapons and how to use them. Only men could touch such sacred items as weapons, for a woman's touch would contaminate them and destroy their efficiency.

After a buffalo hunt each man knew which animals he had killed for each hunter painted his arrows in his own fashion. Arrow shafts were made of various woods—gooseberry, cherry, and juneberry were preferred by the Sioux. The shaft was measured from the elbow to the tip of the little finger, smoothed, and straightened by running it through a flat bone in which a hole had been cut. Three feathers, usually of the turkey buzzard or wild turkey, were cut and attached to the shaft by sinew and glue. After the coming of the white trader, metal points began to replace those made of chipped stone.

Circular shields were made of buffalo hide. The Dakotas covered theirs with buckskin and painted them with designs which had often been revealed to the owner in a vision. Feathers often decorated the shields. As a newly made shield dried in the sun, the lacings holding the cover to the wooden hoop were tightened over a mold, giving the shield a convex shape which helped deflect an arrow.

In an article for *The American West*, magazine of the Western History Association, Francis Haines states:

> To the Plains tribes horses did not bring a new way of living, but a great enrichment of the old way. They still lived off the buffalo, but now they could kill the animals more easily and in greater numbers. They could follow the herds more closely, and could transport larger lodges, more food, and many more personal belongings. Their

adjustments to the new servants were small and easily made.[8]

The period from the coming of the Spaniards in the Southwest during the sixteenth century until the time when most Indians of the Great Plains were placed on reservations in the late nineteenth century has been referred to as "the horse culture period." Historians may differ over the extent to which the horse constituted a major influence upon the culture of the Plains Indians. Walter Prescott Webb states:

> Then came the horse and overnight, so to speak, the whole life and economy of the Plains Indians was changed. Steam and electricity have not wrought a greater revolution in the ways of civilized life than the horse did in the savage life of the Plains.[9]

Clark Wissler, Dean of the Scientific Staff at the American Museum of Natural History, wrote that:

> . . . the importance of the horse lay, not in fighting, but in mobility. Baggage, tents, the aged and children could be transported rapidly. The changes in Indian life brought about by this new mode of travel were even greater than those produced by the automobile in our time.[10]

To Americans, as they moved westward out onto the Great Plains, it appeared that the Indians had been mounted warriors for centuries; they were such excellent horsemen. The first horses had been brought to North America with Coronado's expedition of 1540. Not until the establishment of large

[8] Haines, Francis, "Horses For Western Indians," *The American West* Magazine, Vol. II #2, Spring 1966, p. 14.
[9] Webb, *op. cit.,* p. 53.
[10] Wissler, *Indians of the United States,* p. 262. (© 1940 by Doubleday and Co., Inc. Reprinted with permission of the publisher.)

ranches in northern New Mexico by the Spanish colonists did horses appear in large numbers. The Spanish were well aware of the threat which might be posed by Indians on horseback and thus made it an offense punishable by death for the agricultural Pueblo Indians, who worked the farms and ranches, to possess horses.

From the upper Rio Grande River valley in the vicinity of Sante Fe, the horse culture spread throughout the grasslands of the Great Plains. With the revolt of the Pueblo Indians against the Spanish in 1680, many animals were traded to wild tribes and during the next century the use of horses spread rapidly north until by the time of the American Revolution the Dakota were mounted. The acquisition of horses coincided with the migration onto the Great Plains for these onetime agricultural people.

The horse became a standard of value among the Indians of the Plains. An individual's wealth depended upon the horses he owned. It was traditional that a young man would offer horses in acquiring a bride. In addition, his prestige rose according to the number of horses he presented as gifts to the less fortunate. Of utmost importance, a man's standing as a warrior and his reputation for bravery depended upon his ability in the art of horse stealing.

Warfare among the Plains Indians had different objectives than those of civilized people. The Indian normally went to war for the purpose of gaining revenge, personal glory, or to acquire horses, but rarely to extend dominion over others. The Crow Indians, nomadic neighbors to the west of the Dakota, recognized four categories of personal exploits: (1) Leading a successful war party—one in which no warriors were lost; (2) counting coup upon an enemy (To count coup was to strike a blow upon an enemy); (3) taking a bow from an enemy in hand-to-hand combat; (4) stealing of picketed horses. A chief, who was a distinguished warrior, must have one of each exploit to his credit. One of the most admired acts of personal bravery was the theft of a horse picketed outside the tipi of an enemy warrior. The recovery of stolen horses constituted the major cause for revenge. Indians could break a wild horse in one day, however, they much preferred to steal them from rival tribes after they had been trained.

The Indian was an expert horseman. Indian horses were trained to run next to a fleeing buffalo while the rider, with both hands free, sent arrows into the heart of the animal. While hanging from the back of his horse by one leg, the Indian would throw his bow arm over the horse's neck, and from underneath he would shoot at the enemy with very little of his own body exposed. An Indian warrior could rescue a dismounted friend by reaching down and picking him up by one hand and dragging him to safety.

If, as Frederick Jackson Turner pointed out, the frontier provided a military training school for the frontiersmen, the most competent of instructors were the Indians of the Great Plains. The two great gifts of the white man—the horse and the gun—made the Indian the most formidable of enemies.

> The horse glorified the Plains Indian and brought him a golden age of glory, ease, and conquest which he had never known before. Through long ages the horse has been the symbol of superiority, of victory and triumph. The "man on horseback" rides through the military history of the world; and wherever the horseman appears in statuary or painting he is the central or foremost figure.[11]

By the 1830's the Black Hills and the hunting grounds to the east had become overcrowded as more Sioux moved west across the Missouri. The numbers of buffalo were declining when, in 1834, white traders from the newly constructed Fort William, at the junction of the Platte and Laramie Rivers, appeared in the Sioux villages. One hundred lodges of the Oglalas were persuaded to move south and west of the Black Hills and into the region of the North Platte River near the

[11] Webb, *op. cit.*, p. 493.

fur trading post which was later to be called Fort Laramie. More Sioux were attracted to this region when they learned of the opportunity to trade with the white men and of the great numbers of buffalo to be hunted.

The increasing number of Sioux brought them into conflict with the Crow Indians who had been hunting the Plains east of the Bighorn Mountains. The Crows and the Snake Indians to the west, always friendly to the white trappers and traders, were soon displaced by the aggressive Sioux. Cheyenne and Arapaho Indians, who had hunted the Upper Platte and recently moved south to the Arkansas to live, were counted as allies by the Sioux against their common enemy, the Pawnee. This alliance of Sioux and Cheyenne-Arapaho was maintained in the Indian wars against the whites.

The Intruders

The early associations with the white men often benefited the Sioux who traded horses and buffalo hides for metal tools and weapons. But the fur trade was declining by the early 1840's and the fierce rivalry between competing fur companies for the Indian trade led to uncontrolled use of liquor as a lure to the Indians. The sale of liquor often resulted in demoralization of the Indians. The killing of one Sioux by another had been a rarity; but under the influence of liquor drunken brawls, murder, and quarreling between factions within a band became commonplace.

As the fur trade in the northern Rockies died out, the trappers were soon replaced by newcomers. The first of the Oregon-bound home-seekers, numbering only eighty, passed through Sioux hunting grounds in 1841. This group was overshadowed two years later when the first wagon train of one thousand men, women and children passed by Fort Laramie on their way to Oregon. Mormon pioneers, persecuted and driven from Illinois, rested at Fort Laramie on their way to Salt Lake Valley. Twenty-five thousand gold-seekers bound for California added their numbers to the Oregon and Utah bound settlers. The tide of emigration reached a peak in 1850 when fifty-five thousand emigrants traveled over South Pass in the Rocky Mountains.

The Oregon Trail through the hunting grounds of the Sioux had become a highway; and a treaty with the Indians was needed—one which would guarantee safety to the white emigrants on the Oregon Trail. Accordingly, in 1851, a treaty was signed in which the Indians agreed not to molest wagon trains and to permit the stationing of soldiers along the trail. The government agreed to pay the Indians $50,000 in goods every year and to respect their hunting rights. But good terms between Indians and whites lasted only three years; for the Grattan Massacre of 1854 touched off a war between the Plains Indians and the United States Army which was to last for the next thirty-five years.

The Grattan Massacre, to which a young warrior named Red Cloud was said to have been a witness, resulted from the theft of a Mormon emigrant's cow by a band of Sioux. The Sioux chief reported to the commander at Fort Laramie that the guilty man had been punished, but the commander sent Lieutenant John L. Grattan and thirty men to the Sioux camp to arrest the offender. When the Indians refused to surrender the guilty man, a dispute ensued and the Sioux annihilated Grattan and his entire command.

The arrival of General William S. Harney with a large force of troops quickly crushed growing Sioux opposition to white incursions, and as long as Harney remained the fear of reprisals against them kept the Indians peaceful. General Harney proposed the organization of an Indian police force and the establishment of a tribal government under direction of the United States, but the government refused to consider the plan—one which was years ahead of the Indian policies of that time.

The outbreak of the Civil War in 1861, brought about the removal of federal troops from the frontiers. The following year a major uprising of Santee-Dakotas occurred near their reservation in southwestern Minnesota. Many eastern Dakotas fled west to the country of the Teton and brought stories of the massacres and the hanging of the Indian offenders. Territorial governors demanded that troops be sent from the east while at the same time they were organizing volunteer units from among the frontier settlements. These large numbers of troops helped to bring on the bloody Plains Indian war of 1864. Red Cloud was correct in stating "the white soldiers always want to make war." Life at a frontier post on the Great Plains was monotonous, and the inexperienced and bored soldiers often seized upon any excuse to start a fight with the Indians, most of whom had been friendly toward the whites.

Following the Civil War, railroads began to push west. Cattle ranching was spreading over the grasslands of the Great Plains. Mining communities were springing up in the Rockies. Mining centers such as Helena and Bozeman, in southwestern Montana, had to be supplied from the east; and the most direct route was a proposed road from Fort Laramie on the main overland trail, north to Bozeman and skirting to the east of the Bighorns. The Bozeman Trail was a route familiar to old trappers and traders. It was also a route which cut through the heart of the "Powder River Country," the hunting grounds which had been guaranteed to the Sioux in the treaty of 1851.

The Indians became alarmed as the government sent out surveyors and road-builders. A treaty commission was sent by the government to obtain permission of the Indians to build the road. The commissioners, however, failed to obtain the signatures of the Indians. A meeting was called in 1866 to be held at Fort Laramie. As negotiations proceeded Red Cloud learned that seven hundred soldiers were being led into the Powder River country under the command of Colonel H. B. Carrington. To Red Cloud it appeared that the government was going to build a road through the Indians' hunting grounds and build forts along the road whether the Indians agreed or not. In anger, Red Cloud addressed the treaty makers:

> I will talk to you no more. I will go now, and I will fight you. As long as I live I will fight you. As long as I live I will fight you for the last hunting grounds of my people.[12]

Red Cloud walked out of the meeting and began what was to be referred to as "Red Cloud's War," a war fought in enemy territory against an enemy who was expert in guerrilla warfare and who outmaneuvered United States troops inflicting heavy casualties upon them and finally forcing the United States government to come to terms on conditions laid down by the enemy.

In July of 1866, Colonel Carrington moved his men to the Powder River to begin construction of Fort Phil Kearney. Red Cloud sent word that if the soldiers packed up and left, no harm would come to them. Carrington ordered the area of the fort to be staked out. Then Red Cloud's warriors stampeded part of the soldiers' horse herd. Two soldiers in a rescue party were killed. Within a month, five emigrant trains had been attacked, fifteen people killed. Carrington was forced to ask for reinforcements. When, in August, two companies of soldiers were sent north to the Bighorn River to establish Fort C. F. Smith, the Indians stepped up their harassment of troops at Fort Phil Kearney. Wood trains, sent seven miles into the hills for needed timber had to be heavily guarded; and then, any stray white man was in danger of being killed or captured to be tortured later by the Indians.

Capture by the Indians was the greatest fear of the soldiers. Colonel Richard I. Dodge, an experienced Indian fighter wrote:

> The Indian is thoroughly skilled in all methods of torture, and well knows that that by fire is the

[12] Guinn, "The Red Man's Last Struggle," *Empire* Magazine, p. 8.

most exquisite if it can only be prolonged. He therefore frequently resorts to it when time and opportunity serve. The victim is "staked out" (the man is laid on his back on the ground; his arms and legs, stretched to the uttermost, are fastened by ropes to pins driven into the ground. The victim is not only helpless, but almost motionless.) pleasantly talked to. It is all the best kind of joke. Then a small fire is built near one of his feet. When that is so cooked as to have little sensation, another fire is built near the other foot; then the legs and arms and body, until the whole person has been crisped. Finally, a small fire is built on the naked breast, and kept up until life is extinct.[13]

In November, more reinforcements were sent Carrington. Among them was Captain William J. Fetterman, an infantry officer who held a low opinion of Indians and, like most men recently assigned to the West, was eager for action. In early December, a wood train was attacked, and Captain Fetterman led the rescue party from the fort. The Indians resorted to their usual tactic of fleeing when opposed by superior numbers. Fetterman ordered his men to pursue the Indians. When they were out of sight of the fort, the Sioux turned and attacked Fetterman's command. When Fetterman disappeared from sight, Colonel Carrington took what men could be spared from the fort and rode to his rescue. After the fight, Fetterman was heard to make this statement: "Give me eighty men and I'll ride through the whole Sioux nation."

On Friday morning, December 21, word was received at the fort that the work detail of ninety men sent to gather wood was being attacked. Fetterman volunteered to lead the rescue party. His orders were to relieve the wood train, and under no circumstances to pursue the Indians. Ironically, Fetterman rode out of the fort with eighty men. Ten hand-picked young Sioux warriors rode out in front of Fetterman and his men and lured them into a chase.

[13] Dodge, *33 Years Among Our Wild Indians*, pp. 525–6.

A sign erected by the state of Wyoming records the fate of Fetterman's command:

> Along this ridge on Dec. 21, Brevet Lt. Col. Fetterman, 2 officers, 76 enlisted men and 2 civilians were decoyed into ambush overwhelmed by a superior force of Sioux, Cheyenne and Arapahoe Indians. . . . Fetterman, disobeying orders not to pursue the Indians, issued forth on his ill-fated foray. Although termed a massacre, the fight was actually a pitched battle. The final stand was made behind the large boulders. . . . There were no survivors.[14]

Colonel Carrington, before riding out to relieve Fetterman, gave orders to the undermanned fort that in case of attack, the women and children were to be taken into the powder magazine which was to be blown up in case the fort was overwhelmed. Carrington and his men found every man but six in Fetterman's command to have been killed by arrows, lances, clubs and a few by old muzzle-loading muskets. Only six men had been killed by bullets from guns which were equivalent to those carried by the troops. One body carried 105 arrows!

The Fetterman Massacre emphasized the need to arm and equip troops stationed in the West with weapons better adapted to frontier warfare. In August of 1867, a large force of Sioux and Cheyenne under Red Cloud attacked thirty-two men guarding the wood train sent from Fort Phil Kearney. These few men, armed with new Springfield breech-loading rifles and Colt revolvers, overturned their wagons and prepared a defense-works of wagon boxes. The first charge by 800 Indians was broken up; the second attack and a third attack of over 1200 Indians was stopped before they ever reached the wagon boxes. Indian losses that afternoon numbered between 200 and 300—seven soldiers had been killed.

Although the last battle in Red Cloud's war had been a

[14] Wyo. Historical Marker, U.S. Highway 87, near Banner, Wyo.

defeat for the Indians, they continued their attacks all along the Bozeman Trail. Traffic was brought to a standstill, road-building stopped, and the forts which had been built to protect the road stood useless. The Treaty of 1868 gave Red Cloud what he demanded: the Indians were to retain their hunting grounds in the Powder River country; no whites were to trespass without the Indians' permission, and all the forts built by the sacrifice of many lives were to be abandoned. Before he signed the treaty, Red Cloud was taken on a grand tour of Washington, and it was proposed to the Sioux chief that he settle on a reservation on the Missouri River. Red Cloud made a speech in which he told how the Indians felt:

> When we first had this land we were strong; now we are melting like snow on a hillside, while you are grown like spring grass. Now, I have come a long distance to my Great Father's house. See if I have left any blood in his land when I go. When the white man comes to my country he leaves a trail of blood behind him. . . .
>
> I have two mountains in that country. The Black Hills and the Big Horn Mountain. I want the Father to make no roads through them. I have told these things three times and now I have come here to tell them the fourth. I do not want my reservation on the Missouri. This is the fourth time I have said so. . . .[15]

Red Cloud was settled on a new reservation created for his people on the Platte River near Fort Laramie; but he continued to serve his people, even after the United States government deposed him as a chief for his opposition to the Black Hills Treaty. Red Cloud lived to be an old man. He witnessed the breaking of the Treaty of 1868 by railroad builders surveying a route for the Northern Pacific Railroad on the south side of the Yellowstone River, in the Powder

[15] Guinn, *op. cit.,* p. 11.

River country. Red Cloud witnessed the gold rush to his Black Hills inspired by Colonel George Armstrong Custer's reconnaissance mission into the Black Hills in 1874, which was in violation of the Treaty of 1868.

In 1875, the government ordered the Sioux to leave their Powder River hunting grounds and warned all who did not withdraw to the reservations along the Platte that they would be "deemed hostile and treated accordingly by the military force." This military force was placed under the command of General Crook who had just won victories over the Apache Indians in Arizona. Sitting Bull's Sioux and Cheyenne warriors stopped General Crook in a battle along the Rosebud River in June of 1876. In July of that year, the 100th anniversary of the United States, Custer and two hundred and sixty-four men of the 7th Cavalry were killed in a twenty-minute battle near the banks of the Little Big Horn River in southern Montana.

The defeat of Custer only intensified the demands for placing all the Sioux on reservations. In August of 1876, the government took the Black Hills and sent a treaty commission to negotiate with Red Cloud, Spotted Tail, and other chiefs who were at peace with the white man. The commission reported, in part:

> While the Indians received us as friends and listened with kind attention to our proposition, we were painfully impressed with their lack of confidence in the pledges of the government.
>
> At times they told their story of wrongs with such impressive earnestness that our cheeks crimsoned with shame.[16]

Between 1876 and 1881, eight thousand hostile Sioux, including Sitting Bull and Crazy Horse, gave themselves up and went to live on reservations in South Dakota. Robert M. Utley describes the reservation life of the Sioux in his book:

[16] *Ibid.*, p. 14.

. . . During the following decade, the white man cut the very heart out of the only life they knew. Resentful and suspicious, the old life fresh in their memories, they resisted, not altogether successfully, the substitute offered.

At once, they surrendered a large group of customs on which the old life had focused. Warfare was an activity no longer possible. Planning and conducting raids, performing attendant rituals, celebrating success, and mourning failure had once consumed much of the time, interest, and ambition of the Tetons. Now, except when men gather to reminisce, it consumed none. The principal means of attaining prestige, wealth, and high rank vanished the moment they arrived at the agency. . . .

The tribal economy promptly collapsed. The annual buffalo hunt was no more, not only because officials in Washington regarded it as barbaric but also for the very practical reason that buffalo were growing increasingly scarce. That the vanishing herds symbolized their own vanishing way of life cannot have escaped the Sioux.[17]

In our study of the Indian frontier the emphasis has been upon the Teton-Dakota of the northern Great Plains. No attempt has been made to generalize. We cannot state that the Dakota were typical of all Indians encountered on all frontiers. We can state, however, that Indians were continuously encountered during the westward movement and that misunderstanding, misinterpretation, and mistreatment of the Indian were typical of all frontiers. The late President Kennedy observed that American Indians remain even today the most misunderstood Americans of us all. In his concern for this small segment of our population, he wrote:

American Indians defy any single description. They were and are far too individualistic. They

[17] Utley, *Last Days of the Sioux Nation*, p. 22. (© 1963 by Yale University, by permission of Yale University Press.)

shared no common language and few common customs. But collectively their history is our history and should be part of our shared and remembered heritage. . . .

When we forget great contributors to our American history—when we neglect the heroic past of the American Indian—we thereby weaken our own heritage. We need to remember the contributions our forefathers found here and from which they borrowed liberally.

When the Indians controlled the balance of power, the settlers from Europe were forced to consider their views and to deal with them by treaties and other instruments . . . .

But when the American Indians lost their power, they were placed on reservations, frequently lands which were strange to them, and the rest of the nation turned its attention to other matters.

Our treatment of Indians during that period still affects the national conscience. We have been hampered—by the history of our relationship with the Indians—in our efforts to develop a fair national policy governing present and future treatment of Indians under their special relationship with the Federal government.

Before we can set out on the road to success, we have to know where we are going, and before we can know that we must determine where we have been in the past. It seems a basic requirement to study the history of our Indian people.

America has much to learn about the heritage of our American Indians. Only through this study can we as a nation do what must be done if our treatment of the American Indian is not to be marked down for all time as a national disgrace.[18]

[18] Kennedy, John F., "Introduction," *American Heritage Book of Indians,* p. i. (By permission of American Heritage Publishing Co.)

Bibliography

American Heritage Series	*American Heritage Book of Indians* American Heritage Publishing Company, New York, N.Y.	1961 ed.
Andrist, Ralph K.	*The Long Death* Macmillan, New York, N.Y.	1964 ed.
Dodge, Colonel Richard L.	*Our Wild Indians* Archer House, New York, N.Y.	1956 ed.
Hassrick, Royal B.	*The Sioux, Life and Customs of a Warrior Society* University of Oklahoma Press, Norman, Okla.	1964 ed.
Hyde, George E.	*Red Cloud's Folk, A History of the Oglala-Sioux Indians* University of Oklahoma Press, Norman, Okla.	1937 ed.
Hyde, George E.	*Spotted Tail's Folk, A History of the Brulé-Sioux* University of Okahoma Press, Norman, Okla.	1961 ed.
Jackson, Helen Hunt	*A Century of Dishonor* Harper and Row, New York, N.Y.	1965 ed.
LaFarge, Oliver	*A Pictorial History of the American Indian* Crown Publishers, New York, N.Y.	1956 ed.
Lowie, Robert H.	*Indians of the Plains* Natural History Press, Garden City, N.Y.	1963 ed.
Mayer, Frank H., and Roth, Charles B.	*The Buffalo Harvest* (Sage Books), The Swallow Press, Inc., Chicago, Ill.	1958 ed.
Miller, David Humphreys	*Ghost Dance* Duell, Sloan and Pearce, New York, N.Y.	1959 ed.
National Geographic	*Indians of the Americas* National Geographic, Washington, D.C.	1955 ed.
Underhill, Ruth Murray	*Red Man's America* University of Chicago Press, Chicago, Ill.	1953 ed.
Utley, Robert M.	*The Last Days of the Sioux Nation* Yale University Press, New Haven, Conn.	1963 ed.
Ware, Captain Eugene F.	*The Indian War of 1864* St. Martin's Press, New York, N.Y.	1960 ed.

| Webb,
  Walter Prescott | *The Great Plains*
Blaisdell Publishing Company,
  Waltham, Mass. | 1959 ed. |
| Wissler, Clark | *Indians of the United States*
Doubleday, Garden City, N.Y. | 1940 ed. |

Periodicals

| Guinn, Jack | "The Red Man's Last Struggle,"
  Empire Magazine
The Denver Post, Denver, Colo. | 1966 |
| Haines, Francis | "Horses for Western Indians"
The American West Magazine | 1966 |

3 | The Mountain Men

Frederick Jackson Turner wrote that the frontier strips the garments of civilization from the frontiersman and arrays him in the hunting shirt and the moccasin.

> . . . at the frontier the environment is at first too strong for the man. He must accept the conditions which it furnishes, or perish, and so he fits himself into the Indian clearings and follows the Indian trails. Little by little he transforms the wilderness.[1]

Turner further observed that after reaching the wilderness of the frontier, the white man had adopted the ways of the

[1] Turner, *Significance of the Frontier in American History,* p. 29.

56

Indian even to shouting the war cry and taking a scalp in orthodox Indian fashion.

The Indian trader, the fur trapper, or as he preferred to be called in the West, the mountain man was the vanguard at the frontier. He was the pathfinder. Turner grew up in a part of the country first explored by the *voyageurs,* and he wrote his Master's thesis on "The Influence of the Fur Trader in the Development of Wisconsin." "The Indian trade pioneered the way for civilization," wrote Turner:

> The buffalo trail became the Indian trail, and this became the traders "trace"; the trails widened into roads, and the roads into turnpikes, and these in turn were transformed into railroads.[2]

The Fur Trade

The fur trade was concentrated in the upper Mississippi Valley at the time Lewis and Clark explored the upper Missouri River, the northern Rockies, and the headwaters of the Columbia River from May of 1804 to September of 1806. The journals of Lewis and Clark recorded the possibilities of a profitable fur trade in the West. Only three days after the expedition had departed from its winter camp at the Mandan Indian villages, Lewis wrote:

> at 1 P.M. we overtook three french hunters who had set out a few days before us with a view of traping beaver; they had taken 12 since they left Fort Mandan. these people avail themselves of the protection which our numbers will enable us to give them against the Assinniboins who some- times hunt on the Missouri; and intend ascending with us as far as the mouth of the Yellow stone river and continue there hunt up that river. this is the first essay of a beaver hunter of and discrip-

[2] *Ibid.,* p. 37.

tion on this river. the beaver these people have already taken is by far the best I have ever seen.[3]

Even before Lewis and Clark returned to St. Louis, two men, Joseph Dickson and Forest Hancock set out from Illinois to follow the trail blazed by Lewis and Clark. These two trappers were camped near the mouth of the Yellowstone River when Meriwether Lewis met them on August 12, 1806. They told Clark that they had been hunting and trapping along the Missouri but had, as yet, very little luck in taking beavers; but they were still determined to proceed. Lewis gave them a description of the upper Missouri River and directed them to places where beaver abounded. Three days later, Captain Clark recorded the beginning of the first expedition of mountain men into the wilderness of the Rockies:

> Colter one of our men expressed a desire to join [Dickson and Hancock] who offered to become shearers with [him] and furnish traps &c. the offer [was] a very advantagious one, to him, his services could be dispenced with from this down and as we were disposed to be of service to any one of our party who had performed their duty as well as Colter had done, we agreed to allow him the privilage provided no one of the party would ask or expect a Similar permission to which they all agreed that they wished Colter every suckcess . . . we gave Jo Colter Some Small articles which we did not want and some powder and lead. the party also gave him several articles which will be usefull to him on his expedittion.[4]

John Colter and his companions trapped along the Yellowstone and spent the winter of 1806 and 1807 in what is now southern Montana. In 1808 the first fur trading company of

[3] DeVoto, *Journals of Lewis & Clark,* p. 94.
[4] *Ibid.,* p. 456.

Americans to operate in the Rockies was formed by an experienced trapper of French and Spanish origins, Manuel Lisa. This Missouri Fur Company built Fort Lisa near present-day Omaha in 1812 and this fur trading post remained the most important on the Missouri River until Lisa's death in 1820. Before organizing his company, Lisa employed John Colter and another member of the Lewis and Clark expedition to act as guides and build a fort at the mouth of the Bighorn River. From Fort Manuel, as his first post in the Rocky Mountain region was known, John Colter traveled through wilderness areas bearing the present-day names of Yellowstone Park, Jackson's Hole, and Pierre's Hole on the upper Snake River. Stories of earth which boiled under one's feet, water which spouted out of the ground, valleys steaming with sulphur fumes, and mountains made of glass, resulted in the term "Colter's Hell" being applied to the area. "Out thar in Yellowstone thar's a river that flows so fast it gets hot on the bottom" was one way in which mountain man Jim Bridger described a portion of the beaver country.

Ray Allen Billington, in his study of *The Far Western Frontier* of 1830 to 1860 (p. 41), says of the mountain men:

> Their hour of glory was brief; the trade flourished only between the mid-1820's and the early 1840's. But during those years the fur trappers played a heroic role in opening the land to more permanent settlers. Theirs was the task of spying out fertile valleys that needed only man's touch to yield bountiful harvests, of spreading word of the West's riches throughout the Mississippi Valley, of pioneering routes through mountain barriers, and of breaking down the self-sufficiency of the Indians by accustoming them to the firearms and firewater of civilization. When their day was done all the Far West was readied for the coming of the pioneer farmers.

Billington identifies three jumping-off points where the trappers began their invasions of the beaver country: From Taos,

New Mexico, trappers worked the streams from the Pecos on the east to the Gila on the west and virtually exterminated the beaver from this portion of the Rocky Mountains. From Fort Vancouver on the Columbia River, the men of the Hudson's Bay Company trapped the streams of the Pacific Northwest. St. Louis was the jumping-off point for most American trappers and traders, and credit for opening up the northern Rockies should belong to a group of trappers brought together by General William H. Ashley and his partner Andrew Henry.

Ashley, Lieutenant Governor of the new state of Missouri, brought to the partnership business experience and imagination. Henry had been a member of the American Fur Company's party of Astorians which had followed much the same route of Lewis and Clark in proceeding to the mouth of the Columbia to establish Fort Astoria. The Astorians had camped in the Green River Valley of what is today southwestern Wyoming on their return trip east, and in this valley they had discovered some of the finest beaver country in the west.

On February 13, 1822, the following advertisement appeared in the St. Louis *Missouri Gazette & Public Advertiser*:

To
Enterprising Young Men

The subscriber wishes to engage one hundred men, to ascend the river Missouri to its source, there to be employed for one, two or three years.—For particulars enquire of Major Andrew Henry, near the Lead Mines, in the County of Washington, (who will ascend with, and command the party) or to the subscriber at St. Louis.

Wm. H. Ashley[5]

By 1822 the fur trade had already made St. Louis the largest and busiest town on the frontier, and the successful

[5] From *Jedediah Smith and the Opening of the West* (19–20) by Dale L. Morgan. (By permission of University of Nebraska Press, © 1953.)

rebellion of Mexico against its mother country of Spain in 1821 promised to make St. Louis even more important. William Becknell was preparing a wagon caravan to Santa Fe which would make him "Father of the Santa Fe Trail." Ashley had little difficulty recruiting men for his enterprise. St. Louis' population of 5,000 included boatmen, trappers, traders, soldiers, visiting Indians, farmers, miners, and peddlers. The recruits, for the most part, were young and inexperienced in trapping. Among those who survived the first years were the greatest names in the history of fur trapping in the West.

Jim Bridger, a twenty-year-old barkeeper in St. Louis, "Old Gabe" as he was to be called, established Fort Bridger on the Oregon Trail and helped guide the Mormons into the valley of the Great Salt Lake in the late 1840's.

Thomas Fitzpatrick, a native of Ireland, joined Ashley's band at the age of twenty-four. Fitzpatrick's left hand was shattered from an accidental bursting of his rifle barrel, and the Indians called him "Broken Hand" thereafter. But the Indians also referred to Fitzpatrick as "The man who never lied to us, . . . the best agent we ever had." Fitzpatrick became Indian agent for the tribes on the upper Platte and Arkansas in 1846, and from Bent's Fort he dealt with the Cheyenne, Arapaho and Kiowa justly and fairly. When the first settlers and miners entered the central Rockies these tribes were friendly, thanks to the work of Fitzpatrick.

Louis Vasquez signed on with Ashley when he was twenty-one. A native of St. Louis, his mother was French and his father Spanish. Vasquez spent the remainder of his life in the Rocky Mountains. In 1837 he built Fort Vasquez on the South Platte. Later, he went into partnership with Jim Bridger to build Fort Bridger. When the gold rush of 1859 brought swarms of miners into his old hunting grounds, Vasquez made investments in the new town of Denver.

James Beckwourth, whom Francis Parkman, author of *The Oregon Trail*, described as "a ruffian of the first stamp, bloody and treacherous," became a co-chief of the Crow

Indians and led them against their traditional enemies, the Blackfeet. Beckwourth, a mulatto, had earned the reputation as a tough hombre, a daredevil and a liar, when he narrated his experiences as a mountain man for the book *The Life and Adventures of James P. Beckwourth.* Bernard DeVoto said of the book, it is "one of the gaudiest in our literature and may well be the goriest."

The Sublette brothers gave their name to many locations in the West and added legends to the lore of the mountain man. William Sublette, who with his partners Dave Jackson—for whom Jackson Hole, Wyoming, was named—and Jedediah Smith, bought out Ashley when he retired wealthy from the trapping business. It was William Sublette who brought the first wagons over what would become the Oregon Trail. His brothers, Milton and Andrew, also became prominent in the fur trade.

Perhaps the greatest of all the mountain men, in terms of lasting contributions to the history of the West, was Jedediah Smith. Smith was a relatively old man at twenty-four when he joined Ashley and Henry. He was also as much a greenhorn as any member when he joined, but within a year he was appointed the leader of a brigade of sixteen men sent overland from the Missouri River to the valley of the Green River. In his book *Jedediah Smith and the Opening of the West,* Dale Morgan introduces the reader to the biography of this deeply religious, natural leader of men:

> In the exploration of the American West, Jedediah Strong Smith is overshadowed only by Meriwether Lewis and William Clark. During his eight years in the West Jedediah Smith made the effective discovery of South Pass; he was the first man to reach California overland from the American frontier, the first to cross the Sierra Nevada, the first to travel the length and width of the Great Basin, the first to reach Oregon by a journey up the California coast. He saw more of the West than any man of his time, and was familiar with it

from the Missouri River to the Pacific, from Mexico to Canada. He survived the three worst disasters of the American fur trade, the Arikara defeat of 1823, the Mojave massacre of 1827, and the Umpqua massacre of 1828, in which no less than forty men fell around him, only to die a lonely death on the Santa Fe Trail under the lances of the Comanches.[6]

The object of the mountain man's wanderings was beaver pelt which was much in demand for tall beaver hats, or "stovepipes," so much in fashion through Europe and eastern United States from about 1800 through the early 1840's. Beaver pelts brought an average of four dollars per pound at the trading posts; a pelt would weigh about a pound and a half, thus the standard "six dollars a plew, prime." (A plew was a whole pelt and prime referred to the condition of the pelt.) The best time to trap beaver was when the coat was thick, or "prime" for winter; but since winter trapping was nearly impossible, most pelts were taken in the late fall or early spring.

A brigade of trappers would break up into small parties which would work by themselves for several days. These would break into pairs for the actual trapping, then rejoin the larger party or the brigade to move on to other streams which had not been trapped out. The trapper would usually work upstream when setting his traps because a beaver sign such as tree shavings would float downstream. Signs of other trappers or Indians would also come downstream. Usually the higher the trapper moved into the mountains the safer it became for him.

Traps were set in the late afternoon. The beaver is a nocturnal animal; and by working near dusk, the trapper could avoid warning the beaver of his presence. This also prevented other trappers from discovering the location of one's traps,

[6] From *Jedediah Smith and the Opening of the West* (p. 7) by Dale L. Morgan. (By permission of University of Nebraska Press, © 1953.)

which along with pelts were too valuable to risk being stolen.

The trapper waded into the water to set his traps and when finished, would splash water over his tracks on the bank to eliminate all man-scent. Many mountain men when trapping was poor repeated some ritualistic phrase whose magical effect, they believed, would ensure a good catch. Indians felt that all animals possessed supernatural powers; also that the beaver was among the wisest of animals. Some white men living among Indians could not help being influenced by Indian superstitions.

Beaver pelts were scraped free of flesh and stretched on a round willow frame to dry in the sun for a day or two. When the pelt was dry it was folded with the fur on the inside and marked with the company's symbol or the trapper's name. At the trading post, the pelts were pressed into packs or bales of one hundred pounds for transportation back to St. Louis.

The most factual accounts of the life of a fur trapper in the Rocky Mountains are those of Osborne Russell. Russell was one of the very rare trappers who possessed an education and who documented his travels. He accompanied Nathaniel J. Wyeth's trading caravan to the Rocky Mountains in 1834. The purpose of the expedition was to trade with the men of the Rocky Mountain Fur Company, but the cutthroat competition between men of that company and of the American Fur Company left no market for Wyeth's trade goods. In order to dispose of his merchandise, Wyeth constructed Fort Hall on the Snake River in eastern Idaho. It was from here that Russell began his career which lasted until 1843, and during which time the young trapper maintained his journal which included the following account of the beaver:

> The Beaver . . . is an amphibeous animal but the
> instinct with which it is possessed surpasses the
> reason of a no small portion of the human race.
> Its average size is about 2½ feet long from the
> point of the nose to the insertion of the tail, which

is from 10 to 15 inches long and from 5 to 9 broad flat in the shape of a spade rounded at the corners covered with a thick rough skin resembling scales. the tail serves the double purpose of steering and assisting it thro. the water by a quick up and down motion The hind feet are webbed and the toe next the outside on each has a double nail which serves the purpose of a toothpick to extract the splinters of wood from their teeth as they are the only animals that cut large trees for subsistence . . . . Its color is of light brown generally but I have seen them of a jet black frequently and in one instance I saw one of a light cream color having the feet and tail white The hair is of two sorts the one longer and coarser the other fine short and silky Their teeth are like those of the rat but are longer and stronger in proportion to the size of the animals.[7]

Before setting his traps the mountain man would smear castoreum, or "medicine" as he called it, upon the bank or near the trap to act as bait. The trapper would extract this substance from the beaver and carry it in a small wooden box. The particularly pungent odor of castoreum added to the many other odors accumulated by the typical mountain man. Russell described the process of securing castoreum and using it as bait.

[There are] 4 glands opening forward of the arms two containing oil with which they oil their coats the others containing the castorum a collection of gummy substance of a yellow color which is extracted from the food of the animal and conveyed thro. small vessels into the glands. It is this deposit which causes the destruction of the Beaver by the hunters—When a Beaver Male or female leaves the lodge to swim about their pond they go to the bottom and fetch up some mud between their

[7] From *Journal of a Trapper* (pp. 149–50) by Osborne Russell. (By permission of University of Nebraska Press, © 1955.)

> forepaws and breast carry it on to the bank and
> emit upon it a small quantity of castorum—another
> Beaver passing the place does the same and
> should a hundred Beaver pass within the scent of
> the place they would each throw up mud covering
> up the old castorum and emit new upon that
> which they had thrown up. The Trapper . . . sets
> his trap in the water near the bank about 6 inches
> below the Surface throws a handful of mud on the
> bank about one foot from it and puts a small por-
> tion of the castorum thereon after night the
> Beaver comes out of his lodge smells the fatal bait
> 2 or 300 yds. distant and steers his course directly
> for it he hastens to ascend the bank but the traps
> grasps his foot and soon drowns him . . . .[8]

A trapper's clothing was usually of buckskin, well fringed
at the seams and often highly decorated with beads and porcupine quills. The leather fringes could be used in repairing
clothing, moccasins, and equipment. Buckskin trousers would
become so black and greasy that it was difficult to determine
of what they were made, however. Before trapping season began the trouser legs were often cut short since they would
stretch out of shape from the water, and buffalo skin leggings
were substituted. Stockings were pieces of blanket wrapped
around the feet. The mountain man's shirt was of flannel or
cotton if he was fortunate, if not, antelope skin served the purpose. Moccasins of elk or buffalo skin were usually decorated
with colored beads. Buffalo robes served as blankets and as
heavy coats in cold weather. During the winter, the trapper
wore a fur cap with a brim and flaps which turned down to
protect the trapper's ears; in warm weather he wore an old
felt hat with slouched brim and some had an eagle feather
stuck in the band for good luck. When the clothing became
too covered with vermin, the trapper would lay it across an
ant hill and the vermin would be exterminated by the ants.

Equipment included a riding saddle and bridle, a couple of

[8] *Ibid.*

epishemores which were square pieces of buffalo robe used as saddle blankets, a sack containing six traps, a powder horn slung under one arm by a strap, a leather belt from which hung a bullet pouch, tobacco pouch, and a butcher knife—often a "Green River" knife made popular by the fur traders. The trapper also carried the necessary castoreum in a small wooden box and his "fixens" or "possibles," which included anything he might possibly need such as an awl, flints, and bullet mold, in his "possibles" bag. A hatchet attached to the pommel of his saddle and a rifle completed the outfit. A horse and one or more mules were needed to transport the trapper, his equipment, and his pelts.

Items of necessity, and of luxury—beads, trinkets, sugar—were purchased from the trading posts; the medium of exchange being the "hairy bank notes" as beaver pelts were referred to. The *engagés,* the recruits hired by the fur companies at salaries of $200 to $400 per year, would receive their equipment from the "bourgeois" or chief trader of the fur company. Many of the *engagés* were raw recruits imported from Canada who signed five-year engagements to trap or act as camp tenders. Few of these men completed their contracts. Those who survived blizzards, grizzly bears, Indians, thirst, starvation, or treatment at the hands of such employers as the American Fur Company, either returned to civilization or became "free trappers." Two categories of free trappers were recognized. Those who purchased their outfits on credit from a fur company and who agreed to sell all their pelts to that company alone were known as "skin trappers." The elite of all trappers were those who trapped for themselves wherever they wished and sold their pelts to the company offering the highest price.

Many terms employed by the mountain men were French in origin. *Bourgeois* was soon corrupted by Americans to "booshway." A *cache* was a hiding place. When a trapper lost his horses to the expert Indian horse stealers, he was forced to cache his fixens or pelts in a hollow tree, a cave, or more commonly in a hole dug into the ground which was covered and well concealed. A cache, as well as a scalp, could be "lifted" or "raised." A trapper might refer to himself as "this child"—to refer to another trapper as "old" showed a form of respect. *Fofaraw* was a term used for trinkets, beads, little metal bells, or any decoration of clothing or personal adornment. Indian wives were preferred by the mountain men as white women were too fofaraw for the mountain wilderness; also, they couldn't take care of a camp or make clothing or prepare buffalo meat. An Indian wife was obedient and would accept such punishment as a "lodge-poling" (severe beating) with good grace.

A trapper's speech reflected the type of life he led. On one occasion a group of trappers found a friend's horse and one of them remarked: "Well, it ain't nothin' else, it's the old boy's hoss as sure as shootin' and them Rapahos has rubbed him out at last and raised his animals. Ho, boy! let's lift their hair." In Frederick Ruxton's *Life in the Far West,* Old Bill Williams was quoted as to how to butcher buffalo meat: "do 'ee hyar, now, you darned greenhorn, do 'ee spile fat cow like that whar you was raised? The doin's won't shine in this crowd, boy, do 'ee hyar, darn you? What! butcher meat across the grain! why whar'll the blood be goin' to, you precious Spaniard? Down the grain, I say, and let your flaps be long or out the juice'll run slick, do 'ee hyar now?" [9]

A group of Crow Indians rode into the camp of Osborne Russell and his fellow trappers. Outnumbered and suspicious of the Indians, they decided to leave, and one of the trappers warned the Indians: "If you follow or molest us we will besmear the ground with blood and guts of Crow Indians." [10] Throughout Russell's journal are such statements of mountain wisdom:

> There is a proverb among Mountaineers "That It is better to count ribs than tracks." That is to say

[9] From *Life in the Far West* by George Federick Ruxton. (© 1951 by the University of Oklahoma Press.)
[10] From *Journal of a Trapper* (pp. 56, 71) by Osborne Russell. (By permission of University of Nebrasks Press, © 1955.)

it is better to fasten a horse at night untill you can count his ribs with poverty than turn him loose to fatten and count his tracks after an Indian has stolen him.[11]

The Rendezvous

William Ashley's company, later to become the Rocky Mountain Fur Company, introduced a major refinement to the western fur trade by abandoning the fixed trading post in favor of the rendezvous system. Jedediah Smith suggested to his partner Ashley that the trading company send a caravan of supplies and equipment to the trappers, thus saving the trapper the necessity of proceeding to a distant trading post in order to dispense with his pelts and purchase his necessities. The annual summer rendezvous to be held at a pre-arranged location would save the company the expense of maintaining a permanent trading post.

The first rendezvous was held on Henry's Fork of the Green River in 1825. Ashley's trading party, consisting of twenty-five men, fifty pack horses, one wagon and team, left Fort Atkinson on the Missouri River in November of 1824. The party followed the Platte River to the mountains of northern Colorado, crossed the continental divide at Bridger Pass, and arrived on the Green River in April. Ashley's men, including Tom Fitzpatrick, Jim Clymans, Zacharias Ham, Robert Campbell, and Jim Beckwourth crossed the Great Plains and the Rockies in the most difficult time of the year. Snowstorms, bitter cold winds, scarcity of meat led Beckwourth to write:

> After passing six days without tasting food, the men were weak and disheartened. I listened to all their murmurings and heart-rending complaints. They often spoke of home and friends, declaring they would never see them more. Some spoke of

[11] *Ibid.*

wives and children whom they dearly loved, and
who must shortly become widows and orphans.
They had toiled, they said, through every difficulty; had risked their lives among wild beasts
and hostile Indians in the wilderness, all which
they were willing to undergo; but who could bear
up against actual starvation?

Ashley's men learned from the first rendezvous. The trading caravan for future rendezvous would travel in the spring.
It would bring enough trade goods to supply all of Ashley's
men as well as additional trappers who withdrew from the
employment of the Hudson's Bay Company and others. In
future rendezvous, the traders would be better supplied with
items in demand by trappers and Indians. The first caravan
did not even include a quantity of rum—just sugar, coffee,
tobacco, lead, powder, knives, bar iron and Indian trinkets,
yet this first rendezvous was a financial success as indicated
by an article appearing in the *Missouri Advocate* on October
5, 1825:

Our fellow-citizen, Gen. Ashley, has just returned
from his adventurous enterprize to the Rocky
Mountains, bringing with him one of the richest
cargoes of fur that ever arrived at St. Louis. He
spent the past winter in the bosom of the mountains, and made excursions in the spring down
several of the rivers which go to the Pacific ocean.
The furs obtained by him were brought on horses
to the waters of the Big Horn, where they were
embarked about the middle of Aug. and after a
voyage of three thousand miles arrived at St.
Louis on the 4th inst. It is thus, by the effort of
heroic enterprize, Gen. Ashley has indemnified
himself for all the losses occasioned by the mur-
derous attack of the Arikara's in the summer of
the year 1823.[12]

[12] From *Jedediah Smith and the Opening of the West* (p. 174) by
Dale L. Morgan. (By permission of University of Nebraska Press,
© 1953.)

The article also reported that Ashley had returned with eighty to one hundred packs of beaver pelts valued at between $40,000 and $50,000.

For the next fifteen years, a rendezvous was held somewhere in the vicinity of the Green River in southwestern Wyoming. The last rendezvous took place in 1840 at Horse Creek, near the site of an unsuccessful fur trading post which had been dubbed "Fort Nonsense" by the mountain men.

The scene at a rendezvous was one of gambling, horse racing, wrestling, drinking, storytelling, and general carousing. Men who had been in the mountains away from civilization for months looked forward to the annual rendezvous when they could renew acquaintances, relax, and have a good time. In two weeks or less of riotous living, they managed to spend everything they had received for their pelts, purchase supplies on credit, and returned to the mountains even more in debt to the fur company than before, but with pleasant remembrances to last another year of the fun they had had at the rendezvous. Everything purchased by the trapper was at "mountain prices." The trading companies made a profit of as much as 2,000 percent on articles sold at rendezvous. Mountain prices paid by the trappers as compared to the price the same item would bring in St. Louis are compared:

	Mountain Price	St. Louis Price
Alcohol (diluted)	$5 pint	15¢ gallon
Coffee	$2 pound	15¢ pound
Sugar	$2 pound	9¢ to 13¢ pound
Coarse cloth	$10 yard	14¢ yard (calico)
Flour	$2 pound	2¢ to 3¢ pound
Lead	$2 pound	6¢ pound
Gunpowder	$2 pound	7¢ pound

Osborne Russell described those in attendance at a rendezvous:

> Here we found the hunting Parties all assembled waiting for the arrival of Supplies from the States.

> Here presented what might be termed a mixed
> multitude The whites were chiefly Americans and
> Canadian French with some Dutch, Scotch, Irish,
> English, halfbreed, and full blood Indians, of
> nearly every tribe in the Rocky Mountains.[13]

Gambling took most of the trappers' profit for the year.
Seated in Indian fashion around a fire and with a blanket
spread out before them, the mountain men gambled away
their pelts, mules, rifles, hunting packs, shirts, and breeches.
The gamblers even challenged each other to play for the
highest stakes: the trapper's squaw, if he had one, his horses,
and, as once happened, his scalp. When all his possessions
had been lost, the trapper exclaimed: "There goes hoss and
beaver!" "Hoss and beaver" usually became the possessions
of the fur company's traders.

One of the quickest ways to lose "hoss and beaver" was
the Indian game of "hand."

> A small piece of carved bone . . . was held by the
> gambler, who joining his closed fists together one
> above the other, could thus pass it into either, he
> then separated them and threw his arms wide
> apart, singing and jerking his body up and down,
> and again bringing his hands together, and chang-
> ing or pretending to change the bone, the gamblers
> choosing only when the hands were held wide
> apart. If the guess is right, the guesser pulls away
> his pile with that of the bone holder.[14]

Indians outnumbered whites in attendance at the rendez-
vous. Lodges, and sometimes whole villages of Crow, Snake,
Nez Percé, Bannock, Flathead, and perhaps a few Teton-
Sioux, Utes and Cheyenne camped along the tributary streams

[13] From *Journal of a Trapper* (p. 58) by Osborne Russell. (By permission of University of Nebraska Press, © 1955.)
[14] DeVoto, *Across the Wide Missouri*, p. 98.

of the Green, the Snake, and the Wind Rivers. Anxious to trade beaver pelts, buffalo robes, and horses (usually stolen from other Indians or from trappers themselves) for beads, hatchets, kettles, and all too often for liquor. The liquor used in trading was well diluted and the traders made certain that Indians received less than full measure. Often, fat was melted and placed into the bottom of a tin cup. A thumb (or even all four fingers) was occasionally thrust into the cup which cheated the Indians who were unable to detect the shortage. Ruxton observed that the traders set to work immediately to induce the Indians to trade:

> In opening a trade a quantity of liquor is first given "on the prairie", as the Indians express it in words, or by signs in rubbing the palm of one hand quickly across the other, holding both flat. Having once tasted the pernicious liquid, there is no fear but they will quickly come to terms; and not unfrequently the spirit is drugged, to render the unfortunate Indians still more helpless. Sometimes, maddened and infuriated by drink, they commit the most horrid atrocities on each other, murdering and mutilating in a barbarous manner, and often attempting the lives of the traders themselves.[15]

The most enjoyable aspect of the rendezvous, to most of the trappers, was the conversation, the swapping of stories around the fire at night. Few of the stories told by mountain men have been preserved in American folklore as have the legends of rivermen, lumberjacks, and cowmen. The average trapper was illiterate, and he appreciated the rare instances when someone like Jed Smith would read aloud from the Bible. Jim Bridger loved to listen to someone read the classics and remarked that Shakespeare, in writing of the murder of two young princes, must "have had a bad heart

[15] From *Life in the Far West* (p. 99) by George Frederick Ruxton. (© 1951 by the University of Oklahoma Press.)

and been as devilish mean as a Sioux, to have written such scoundrelism as that." *Across the Wide Missouri* (p. 45) is one of the finest accounts of the last years of the fur trade and Bernard DeVoto gives this description of the yarn-spinning of the mountain men:

> It was shop talk, trapping, hunting, trailing, fighting Indians, escaping from Indians, the lore of animals and plants, and always the lay of the land and old fields revisited and new fields to be found, water and starvation and trickery and feasts. How Long Hatcher had lifted those Apache scalps. How one who was with us last year was eviscerated by a grizzly or gutshot by a Blackfoot. How Old Gabe outsmarted a Blackfoot war party, or Tom Fitzpatrick lay in his crevice while the Gros Ventres looked for him, or a Delaware . . . had taunted the Arikaras who were killing him piecemeal. How one's partner had wandered into a canyon quite unknown even to these masters of geography, how another had stolen the daughter of a Sioux medicine man or a Taos rancher, how a third had forted up behind his slaughtered horse and held off fifty Comanches. How we came into Taos or the Pueblo of Los Angeles and the . . . brandy we drank and the horses we stole.

His pelts traded, his money spent, outfitted with a new string of traps, and with a fresh supply of tobacco, powder, and lead, the trappers departed the rendezvous. Travelling in groups, or in pairs, or singly, they headed back to the mountains to search out new beaver grounds, to hole up for the winter in some isolated valley, and to return in the summer —if they were lucky—to the next rendezvous.

Primitive Existence

To a greater extent than any other group of pioneers, the mountain men reverted to the most primitive existence. For much of his life he lived in an environment completely cut off from all contacts with civilization; in order to survive, the mountain man was forced to adapt himself to an environment of nature and not of man. Enemies were everywhere, and the trapper had to be constantly on the alert. He was completely on his own, his food and water supply depended upon his ability to secure them; any injury which he or his animals might sustain had to be treated by the mountain man himself; he had to provide his own clothing, repair his own equipment, build his own shelters and secure his own firewood in a country often barren of timber. The successful trapper, the one who survived, quickly learned to adopt the ways of the Indian. He resorted to the savagery of the Indian and became as cruel as the most barbarous of Indians. His eating habits became those of the Indian; his language was influenced by that of the Indian. Like the Indian the mountain man's entire mental attitude was one of callousness toward hardships and of acceptance of death as commonplace.

In leading a war party of Crow Indians against a party of Blackfoot Indians, a trapper was seen cutting off the hands of the wounded enemy and gouging out their eyes. In more than one instance trappers who were starving were known to have resorted to cannibalism. The story is told of "Cannibal Phil" who was lost in a winter blizzard but reappeared in camp with the leg of his Indian companion packed on his mule; throwing the leg to the ground, Phil was reputed to have said: "There, I won't have to gnaw on you any more."

A mountain man was as expert in taking a scalp as any Indian warrior. Taking a firm hold of the scalp with one hand, he would make two semicircular incisions on either side, loosen the skin with his knife, and place his feet against the dead man's shoulders until the scalp pulled loose.

At the rendezvous of 1829, held at Pierre's Hole on the Snake River, a trapper had purchased a small kettle of alcohol and passed it around the campfire. After the kettle had made several rounds, one of them seized it and poured the contents over another trapper, then picking up a lighted stick, he touched it to the other's clothing.

The battle at Pierre's Hole in 1832 occurred when a large number of trappers who had just left the rendezvous, ran into an entire village of Gros Ventre Indians, who were on their way to the country of their allies, the Blackfoot Indians. During the battle both sides "forted up" and neither group could dislodge the other. The mountain men decided that the best way to take care of the Gros Ventre was to set fire to the surrounding dry grass and brush. But Indian allies of the mountain men argued against burning the enemy to death not because of any feeling of humanity toward their enemy but, because too much valuable loot would also be burned up in the process. In this one instance practicality won out over savagery.

As did the Indians, the mountain men gorged themselves on meat when the hunting was good. When they had plenty, they ate the best pieces first for fear "of being killed by some brat of an Indian before we have enjoyed them . . ." The best pieces of the buffalo were the hump ribs which were given a peppery flavor by being roasted over a fire of buffalo chips. Warm buffalo blood reminded the mountain men of fresh milk. The liver, flavored by the contents of the full bladder, was eaten raw. Bones were cracked, and the marrow extracted. Meat was pulled off the ribs and gulped down while grease dripped off the trapper's chin and ran down his clothing. From time to time he might wipe his hands on his clothing or his long hair, but continue eating until he had devoured about eight or nine pounds of buffalo meat.

Frederick Ruxton wrote of watching two Canadian trappers eating buffalo intestines, or *"boudins"*; they commenced:

> at either end of such a coil of grease, the mass lying between them on a dirty apishemore like the coil of a huge snake. As yard after yard glided glibly down their throats, and the serpent on the saddle-cloth was dwindling from an anaconda to a moderate-sized rattlesnake, it became a great

point with each of the feasters to hurry his operation, so as to gain a march upon his neighbor and
improve the opportunity by swallowing more than
his just proportion; each at the same time exhort-
ing the other, whatever he did, to feed fair and
every now and then, overcome by the unblushing
attempts of his partner to bolt a vigorous mouthful,
would suddenly jerk back his head, drawing out
at the same moment, by the retreating motion,
several yards of *boudin* from his neighbor's
stomach and, snapping up the ravished portions,
greedily swallowed them.[16]

But when food was scarce "meat was meat," as the trapper
said, and he would eat anything—boiled beaver tail, his own
moccasins, young puppy dog, or the ears off his own mule.
During "starvin' " times a trapper might bleed his horse and
drink the blood. One trapper held his hands over an ant hill
until they were covered with ants, then "greedily licked them
off." And, like the Digger Indians of the Great Basin, trappers would gather large black crickets, throw them into a
kettle of boiling water, and when they stopped kicking,
would eat them.

Even when meat was available, lack of firewood or a
storm might make preparation of it difficult. Such was the
instance described by Osborne Russell:

We sat down round the fire with each holding a
piece of beef over it on a stick with one hand
while the other was employed in keeping up the
blaze by feeding it with wet sage and weeds until
the meat was warmed thro. when it was devoured
with an observation that "Bull Meat was dry eating when cooked too much." After supper (if I
may be allowed to disgrace the term by applying
it to such a Wolfish feast) we spread the Bull skin
down in the mud in the dryest place we could find

16 From *Life in the Far West* (p. 41) by George Frederick Ruxton.
(© 1951 by the University of Oklahoma Press.)

and laid down upon it. Our fire was immediately put out by the rain . . . We lay tolerably comfortable whilst the skin retained its animal warmth and remained above the surface but the mud being soft the weight of our bodies sunk it by degrees below the water level which ran under us on the skin but we concluded it was best to lie still and keep the water warm that was about us . . . .[17]

The trapper became used to such hardships, and when he suffered from attacks of arthritis, the mountain man accepted these as a natural result of wading around in icy streams to set his traps. The attack of a huge grizzly bear upon Jedediah Smith would have killed a lesser man, but the incident offers an example of the mountain man's acceptance of misfortune and his toleration of pain. Such was the attitude as described by Smith's companion, Jim Clyman:

Grissly did not hesitate a moment but sprang on the capt taking him by the head first pitc[h]ing sprawling on the earth he gave him a grab by the middle . . . breaking several of his ribs and cutting his head badly none of us having any sugical Knowledge what was to be done one Said come take hold and he wuld say why not you so it went around I asked the Capt what was best he said one or 2 [go] for water and if you have a needle and thread git it out and sew up my wounds around my head which was bleeding freely I got a pair of scissors and cut off his hair and then began my first Job of d[r]essing wounds upon examination I [found] the Bear had taken nearly all his head in his capcious mouth close to his left eye on one side and close to his right ear on the other and laid the skull bare to near the crown of the head leaving a white streak whare his teeth passed one of his ears was torn

[17] From *Journal of a Trapper* (p. 75) by Osborne Russell. (By permission of University of Nebraska Press © 1955.)

from his head out to the outer rim after stitching
all the other wounds in the best way I was capable
and according to the captains directions the ear
being the last I hold him I coud do nothing for
his Eare. O you must try to stitch up some way or
other said he then I put in my needle stiching it
through and through and over and over laying the
lacerated parts togather as nice as I could with my
hands . . . .[18]

Though Jed Smith recovered from his wounds, other mountain men were less fortunate. It mattered little whether a
man died from the grizzly's claws, an Indian's arrows, or a
blizzard, his death was accepted with little comment and less
mourning by his companions. Each man knew that death was
to be expected as part of the kind of life he led. "Poor fellow!
Out of luck" was the usual reaction to a friend's death.

The mountain man's speech took on the elements of that
of the Indians. A trapper's "wagh" was the equivalent of the
Indians' "ugh" and indicated agreement or approval. The
trapper's voice was also usually high pitched, like that of the
Indian, and their manner of emphasizing each spoken syllable
reflected the Indian pattern of speech.

Indian names for geographic places were colorful and
descriptive. So, too, were place names applied by trappers:
Hell Roaring Creek, Stinkingwater River, Sweetwater Valley,
Sunlight Basin, Medicine Lodge, Two-Ocean Pass, Beaver-
head Rock, and the Bighorn Mountains. Water dirtied by
the fine sand blown into it by the wind, so muddy that it was
scarcely drinkable, gave Powder River its name.

By the late 1830's, few beaver were left in the western
mountains. Every valley and river had been explored and
trapped by the mountain men. They had become familiar
with every geographic feature, every Indian trail, and every
mountain pass. When the silk topper replaced the beaver hat
as the fashionable head-wear, the era of the mountain man

[18] From *Jedediah Smith and the Opening of the West* (p. 84) by Dale
L. Morgan. (By permission of University of Nebraska Press, © 1953.)

was at an end. Few of the trappers returned to "the States," preferring instead to hunt buffalo or guide emigrant trains, or scout for American armies in the Mexican War. The exploration of these first pathfinders, their knowledge of the West, and their service in opening the frontier to settlement, contributed to the achievement of our "Manifest Destiny."

The character of the mountain man is portrayed in the following excerpt from Osborne Russell's *Journal of a Trapper*:

> Here [on the Platte] we had plenty of wood water meat and dry grass to sleep on, and taking everything into consideration we thought ourselves comfortably situated—comfortably I say for mountaineers not for those who never repose on anything but a bed of down or sit or recline on anything harder than Silken cushions for such would spurn at the idea of a Hunter's talking about comfort and happiness but experience is the best Teacher hunger good Sauce and I really think to be acquainted with misery contributes to the enjoyment of happiness and to know ones self greatly facilitates the Knowledge of Mankind— One thing I often console myself with and that is the earth will lie as hard upon the Monarch as it will on a Hunter and I have no assurance that it will lie upon me at all, my bones may in a few years or perhaps days be bleaching on the plains in these regions like many of my occupation without a friend to turn even a turf upon them after a hungry wolf has finished his feast.[19]

[19] From *Journal of a Trapper* (p. 76) by Osborne Russell. (By permission of University of Nebraska Press, © 1955.)

Bibliography

Beckwourth, James P.	*The Life and Adventures of James P. Beckwourth* Harper, New York, N.Y.	1856
Billington, Ray Allen	*The Far Western Frontier* Harper, New York, N.Y.	1956 ed.
Bingham, Edwin	*The Fur Trade in the West* D. C. Heath, Boston, Mass.	1960 ed.
DeVoto, Bernard	*Across the Wide Missouri* Houghton Mifflin, Boston, Mass.	1947 ed.
DeVoto, Bernard	*The Journals of Lewis and Clark* Houghton Mifflin, Boston, Mass.	1953 ed.
Ewers, John C.	*Adventures of Zenas Leonard, Fur Trader* University of Oklahoma Press, Norman, Okla.	1959 ed.
Favour, Alpheus Hoyt	*Old Bill Williams* University of Oklahoma Press, Norman, Okla.	1962 ed.
Field, Matthew C.	*Matt Field on the Santa Fe Trail* University of Oklahoma Press, Norman, Okla.	1960 ed.
Garrard, Lewis	*Wah-to-yah and the Taos Trail* University of Oklahoma Press, Norman, Okla.	1955 ed.
Garst, Doris	*Jim Bridger: Greatest of the Mountain Men* Houghton Mifflin, Boston, Mass.	1952 ed.
Gregg, Josiah	*Commerce of the Prairie* University of Oklahoma Press, Norman, Okla.	1954 ed.
Hafen, LeRoy	*The Mountain Men and the Fur Trade of the Far West* Arthur H. Clark Company, Glendale, Calif.	1965 ed.
Lavendar, David	*The Fist in the Wilderness* Doubleday, Garden City, N.Y.	1964 ed.
Lavendar, David	*Bent's Fort* Doubleday, Garden City, N.Y.	1954 ed.
Lavendar, David	*Trail to Santa Fe* Houghton Mifflin, Boston, Mass.	1958 ed.
Lent, Geneva D.	*West of the Mountains* University of Washington Press, Seattle, Wash.	1963 ed.

81

Mayer, Frank H., and Roth, Charles B.	*Buffalo Harvest* (Sage Books) The Swallow Press, Inc. Chicago, Ill.	1958 ed.
Morgan, Dale L.	*Jedediah Smith and the Opening of the West* University of Nebraska Press, Lincoln, Neb.	1953 ed.
Oglesby, Richard	*Manuel Lisa and the Opening of the Missouri Fur Trade* University of Oklahoma Press, Norman, Okla.	1963 ed.
Phillips, Paul Chrisler	*The Fur Trade* University of Oklahoma Press, Norman, Okla.	1961 ed.
Porter, Mae Reed	*Scotsman in Buckskin* Hastings House, New York, N.Y.	1963 ed.
Rawling, Gerald	*The Pathfinders* Macmillan, New York, N.Y.	1964 ed.
Ross, Alexander	*The Fur Hunters of the West* University of Oklahoma Press, Norman, Okla.	1956 ed.
Russell, Osborne	*Journal of a Trapper* University of Nebraska Press, Lincoln, Neb.	1955 ed.
Ruxton, George Frederick	*Life in the Far West* University of Oklahoma Press, Norman, Okla.	1959 ed.
Sandoz, Mari	*The Beaver Men* Hastings House, New York, N.Y.	1964 ed.
Skinner, Constance Lindsay	*Adventure of Oregon* Yale University Press, New Haven, Conn.	1920 ed.
Vestal, Stanley	*Kit Carson, the Happy Warrior of the Old West* Houghton Mifflin, Boston, Mass.	1928 ed.

4 | The Prospectors

The various frontiers in America's history have made similar contributions to the American character. "But with all these similarities," observed Frederick Jackson Turner, "there are essential differences, due to the place element and the time element." As an example, Professor Turner compared the farming frontier of the Mississippi Valley with the very different conditions of the mining frontier of the Rocky Mountains.

What were the conditions of the Western mining camps which were so different from those of the farmer's frontier? Was there a difference between the Forty-Niners "gold fever" and the Oregon-bound emigrant's "land hunger"? Were these frontiersmen, the miners, the farmers, and the trappers before them, exhibiting in different forms, "that restless, nervous energy" which Turner stated was a trait of the frontier? Perhaps the discoveries of gold in 1848 at Sutter's mill, in the Pike's Peak region a decade later, and in the Black Hills in 1874, created such a desire to get rich quick that mass migration to unpopulated regions was a natural result. Perhaps, too, these discoveries of gold simply provided excuses to "see the elephant," as the Forty-Niner or Pikes Peaker referred to the trait identified by Turner as frontier inquisitiveness.

Most certainly, the miner exhibited what Turner referred to as a "practical, inventive turn of mind" when, in the absence of adequate mining implements, he invented and built his own. But to what extent did the frontier trait of "dominant individualism" influence the conduct of miners' meetings and the creation of mining districts which became the basis for government in the frontier mining camps? In breaking the bonds of custom, what new institutions were established in the miners' "diggings"? These are but a few questions to be raised in a study of the miner's frontier.

In an 1838 speech to the United States Senate, Daniel Webster gave expression to many an Easterner's attitude toward the far West, particularly the far Southwest, when he remarked:

> What do we want with this vast worthless area, this region of savages and wild beasts, of deserts, shifting sands and whirlwinds of dust, of cactus and prairie dogs? To what use could we ever hope to put these great deserts or those endless mountain ranges, impregnable and covered to their very base with eternal snow? What use have we for such a country?
>
> . . . I shall never vote one cent from the public treasury to place the Pacific Coast one inch nearer Boston than it is now.[1]

[1] From *The First Hundred Years* (p. 12) by Robert L. Perkin. (© 1959 by the Denver Publishing Co. By permission of Doubleday and Co., Inc.)

By 1846, the year in which the war with Mexico began, many Americans still shared Webster's opinion of the far West. New England's hide and tallow traders were familiar with the Spanish missions and the large ranches. Some fur trappers eventually settled in valleys of California where they had once sought beaver. Still, few Americans occupied the scattered farms, ranches, and orchard lands of California. Americans preferred, instead, the Oregon country where the land and climate were more similar to the older frontiers of the nation.

California and the Mexican Cession were acquired by the treaty of Guadalupe-Hidalgo signed on January 2, 1848, near Mexico City. Three weeks later, an event took place on the huge estate of John Augustus Sutter, near present-day Sacramento, which was to convert California from a near wilderness to statehood in slightly over two years. Sutter, to whom the Mexican government had granted a tract of land measuring nearly 150 square miles, described that event:

> I was sitting one afternoon just after my siesta, engaged . . . in writing a letter to a relation of mine at Lucern [Switzerland, from which Sutter had come], when I was interrupted by Mr. Marshall, a gentleman with whom I had frequent business transactions—bursting into the room. From the unusual agitation in his manner I imagined that something serious had occurred, and, as we involuntarily do in this part of the world, I at once glanced to see if my rifle was in its proper place. You should know that the mere appearance of Mr. Marshall at that moment in the Fort, was quite enough to surprise me, as he had but two days before left the place to make some alterations in a mill for sawing pine planks, which he had just run up for me some miles higher up the Americanos [River]. When he had recovered himself a little, he told me that, however great my surprise might be at his unexpected reappearance, it would

be much greater when I heard the intelligence he
had come to bring me. "Intelligence," he added,
"which if properly profited by, would put both of
us in possession of unheard-of wealth—millions
and millions of dollars, in fact." I frankly own,
when I heard this that I thought something had
touched Marshall's brain, when suddenly all my
misgivings were put at an end by his flinging on
the table a handful of scales of pure virgin gold.[2]

In widening the tailrace of Sutter's mill, Marshall had discovered the gold. Telling no one of his discovery, he rode
the forty miles to Sutter's fort with the news which would
bring hordes of gold-seekers onto Sutter's lands.

At first, only a few individuals were attracted to the site
of the initial discovery. Some of these first prospectors were
members of the Mormon Battalion which had been recruited
by President Polk to fight in the Mexican War. After the
Mormon Battalion had disbanded, most of the members
made their way back to the Mormon settlements in Utah. A
few stayed behind, however, including those who prospected
up the South Fork of the American River. According to
tradition, news of success at these Mormon diggings was
brought to San Francisco by a prominent merchant of that
town, Sam Brannan. Brannan was said to have rushed
through the plaza shouting, "Gold! Gold! Gold! from the
American River." For proof he displayed a bottle of gold
dust to the excited onlookers.

The Forty-Niners

Within a month, San Francisco was all but de-populated
as its inhabitants abandoned homes, shops, and even schools,
in their rush to the Sierras. Sailors deserted their ships in
San Francisco harbor; men from Oregon abandoned the
farms they had traveled 2,000 miles to claim. Mexicans from

2 Peters, *California on Stone,* pp. 67–69.

Sonora, and Kanakas from the Hawaiian Islands, joined the five thousand Californians and Oregonians to wash over five million dollars worth of gold dust out of the Sacramento River and its tributaries in 1848. News of gold strikes on the Sacramento spread rapidly through the States, and by the next year the "rush of '49" was under way.

The presence of gold in California was given official recognition by President Polk himself and even the most cautious of would-be prospectors were caught up in the fever. The president informed Congress in December of 1848 that the abundance of gold in California territory would scarcely command belief. By mid-summer of 1849, over forty thousand "argonauts" were on the overland trails headed for the "diggings." By 1850, as many as eighty thousand gold-seekers reached California by way of the Oregon, California, Santa Fe, or other trails, some of which crossed northern Mexico. As many as thirty-five thousand men reached California by ship, either by way of the Cape Horn route, or to Panama where they crossed the Isthmus and awaited ships on the Pacific side.

Those who could afford both the time and expense of the Cape Horn route preferred it for its relative comfort and safety. The Panama route was favored by individuals who wanted, for one reason or another, to beat the crowds to the gold fields. Gamblers, speculators, businessmen, and politicians usually favored the quickest possible route. One such Forty-Niner was Bayard Taylor, a twenty-four-year-old writer for the *New York Tribune*. Arriving on the Pacific side of the Isthmus, Taylor found nearly three hundred men competing for the fifty-two available steamship passages to California. A few months before, there were three thousand men awaiting passage on a ship of any kind.

Many of the ships were not seaworthy. Conditions were crowded and dirty. Food was often ill-prepared and sometimes in short supply. Taylor wrote of his voyage:

Our vessel was crowded fore and aft: exercise was

rendered quite impossible and sleep was each night a new experiment, for the success of which we were truly grateful. We were roused at daylight by the movements on deck, if not earlier, by the breaking of a hammock-rope and the thump and yell of the unlucky sleeper . . . . The breakfast hour was nine, and the table was obliged to be fully set twice. At the first tingle of the bell, all hands started as if a shot had exploded among them; conversation was broken off in the middle of a word; the deck was instantly cleared, and the passengers, tumbling pell-mell down the cabin-stairs, found every seat taken by others who had probably been sitting in them for half an hour . . . . There was a confused grabbing motion for a few seconds, and lo! the plates were cleared. A chicken parted in twain as if by magic, each half leaping into an opposite plate; a dish of sweet potatoes vanished before a single hand; beef-steak flew in all directions . . . .[3]

While the Panama route was quickest, taking six to eight weeks, the overland routes were most popular because overland travel required the least expenditure of money. Many a farm boy from the Mississippi Valley reached California on physical strength, determination, a wagon and oxen borrowed from his family and a few dollars' worth of food and hand tools. Planning and organization characterized some journeys to the gold fields, however. "Stock companies" were organized in the East, and even in Europe, to combine resources, purchase a ship, equipment, and food necessary for the voyage. Once in the gold fields, members intended to share their profits.

Most Forty-Niners followed the trail established by the Oregon pioneers, usually to a point beyond Fort Hall in what is now Idaho. From the Snake River to the Sacramento, they

[3] Taylor, Bayard, *Eldorado: or Adventures in the Path of Empire.* New York, 1850 as quoted in Angle, Paul, *The American Reader,* Rand McNally, 1958, p. 251.

encountered obstacles not included in such popular guide-books of the day as Lansford Hastings' *Emigrants' Guide* and John C. Fremont's *Report of the Exploring Expedition to the Rocky Mountains in 1842*. A later guide book (pp. 324–5) gave the following advice:

> We would recommend emigrants who have cattle to shoe them, and we would advise, not to take them further on the route than Fort Hall, or Great Salt Lake, but exchange them there for others, or horses. It is useless for men to start from either of these places with worn out cattle, as they never will get them to their journey's end . . . . The road from the States to Salt Lake or Fort Hall, is comparatively a railroad to the one from thence to California. We would recommend no man to over-load his wagon with tools, &c., for spades, shovels, picks, &c., can be purchased cheap in California. Throw away your old yokes, chains, boxes, &c., for you will do so before you cross the desert, no wagon should have more than 800 lbs. with three yoke of cattle.
>
> . . . Pack animals are the best all the time, and single men had by all means better pack. Hard bread is the best to take from either of these places; also dried beef.
>
> Clothes can be bought in Sacramento and Stockton, as cheap as in the States, and it is useless for men to overload themselves with such articles, to retard their movements . . . . Men carrying ploughs, anvils, gold washers, stoves, or any other article of weight, may as well throw them away, or dispose of them; as it is perfectly useless to wear out their cattle, and at last leave the cattle, and goods between this [Salt Lake City] and California.
>
> After the emigrant settles on his winter diggins, he had better secure provisions enought to last him until April; together with pickles, vinegar, etc. as a preventive to the scurvy.

> Emigrants had better not dispose of their animals when they are poor, but place them in good hands on ranches; as a poor horse or ox will not fetch over $10 or $15, while a fat ox or horse is worth $100.[4]

The dangers which resulted from deviating from established routes are emphasized in the following reflections (pp. 54–5):

> Came from Iowa to Calif. in '49 across the plains in ox teams, 7 Mo Enroute—with 64 wagons—All went well till we reached Salt Lake—It being late in the season we concluded to winter at Utah Fort but learning that the Mormons were about to attack us we broke camp and with a Mexican guide took the south route for Los Angeles which was the pioneer train over that route being 5 days at times going 3 Miles. At Santa Clara Canyon the Indians ran off 9 head Cattle and shot one full of arrows—We surprised one of the braves who had his bow bent to fire on us by shooting him on the spot, which threw the enemy into disorder and so we escaped further trouble—Soon after leaving this place we ran short of provisions and my brother and myself started in pursuit of rations—Instead of reaching the settlements in 3 days we were 13 days and for 3 days and nights had nothing to eat . . . .[5]

The author failed to explain what his party had done to provoke the Mormons into an attack upon their train. It was noted, however, that upon arrival in California he engaged in mining where he made "plenty of money." The account concluded (p. 55):

> In coming into Cal. I came as a poor boy and what fortune I have at the present was made by hard labor and industrious habits—being perfectly temperate all my life.[6]

[4][5][6] From *Journals of Forty-Niners* by LeRoy R. and Ann W. Hafen. (By permission of The Arthur H. Clark Co.)

Being both successful as a miner and temperate in his habits might have distinguished the Forty-Niner just quoted from most of his companions in the diggings. California society was decidedly masculine during the first years of the gold rush, and most of the men were under forty years of age. In the spring of 1849 there were only fifteen women in San Francisco, California's largest city. So few were the numbers of "home-like" ladies in those early months that one seventeen-year-old miner rode thirty-five miles just to see a miner's wife recently arrived in a nearby district. The young man was reminded of home when, after sewing on a button, the woman admonished him for gambling and drinking.

The mines of the "Mother Lode" district placed all men on the same level. Family background, manners, style of dress or speech, these things mattered little in the mining regions. One might be the richest man in camp and not be able to hire a servant because those who had been servants were working their own claims. Every man had the same start, and the least experienced miner of the camp might suddenly strike it rich.

Observers differed in their opinions of the character of California's mining society.

> Take a sprinkling of sober-eyed, earnest, shrewd, energetic New-England business-men: mingle with them a number of rollicking sailors, a dark band of Australian convicts and cut-throats, a dash of Mexican and frontier desperadoes, a group of hardy back-woodsmen, some professional gamblers, whiskey-dealers, general swindlers, or "rural agriculturists" . . . and having thrown in a promiscuous crowd of broken-down merchants, disappointed lovers, black sheep, unfledged dry-goods clerks, professional miners from all parts of the world . . . stir up the mixture, season strongly with gold-fever, bad liquors, faro, monte, rouge-et-noir, quarrels, oaths, pistols, knives, dancing,

and digging, and you have something approximating to California society in early days.[7]

Charles Howard Shinn was born in California during the gold rush. As a young man he became well-acquainted with mining communities through teaching school in a number of them. His book *Mining Camps A Study in American Frontier Government* (pp. 134–5), defends the miner as an organizer of society, a New World Viking or crusader:

> He often appears in literature as a dialect-speaking rowdy, savagely picturesque, rudely turbulent: in reality, he was a plain American citizen cut loose from authority, freed from the restraints and protections of law, and forced to make the defence and organization of society a part of his daily business.

Mining Techniques

The early gold discoveries in California, the Pikes Peak region, Black Hills, or any of the many areas which experienced gold rushes, were located in placer deposits. These deposits were located near the surface, in stream beds, or in the banks along the side of a gulch. Placer mining consisted, basically, of separating the gold from the gravel, clay, or dirt in which it was found. Such gold, found in an almost pure state, was termed "free gold" and ranged in size from nuggets to powder-like "flour gold."

The experienced miner, of whom there were very few, knew that gold originated in lodes or veins which were streaks of mineral-bearing rock extending down into the earth for long distances. To recover gold from a lode or vein required heavy equipment to crush the mineral-bearing rock and separate it from the gold, but the ore itself had to be mined from

[7] Shinn, *Mining Camps,* p. 158.

92

tunnels far below the surface. Such hard-rock mining required large expenditures of capital and the first miners into any district arrived with the simplest of equipment and employed the simplest of methods. The popular song of the day indicated the extent to which many Forty-Niners could afford to equip themselves:

> Oh, California, that's the land for me;
> I'm going to Sacramento
> With my washbowl on my knee!

But what these prospectors lacked in tools and experience they possessed in optimism:

> I'll scrape the mountains clean, my boys,
> I'll drain the rivers dry,
> A pocketful of rocks bring home,
> So brothers, don't you cry.

The first methods employed were those of placer mining. The gold pan was the simplest tool and the easiest to operate. The pan was circular in shape, ten to eighteen inches in diameter, with sloping sides, and made of sheet iron. The prospector placed gravel or dirt in the pan, filled it with water from a stream which helped break up the lumps of dirt or clay, throwing out the larger pebbles. Then, holding the pan with both hands just below the surface, he would shake the pan from side to side. Any gold in the pan would be carried to the bottom because of its weight. Then, with a circular motion, the miner would wash the lighter sands and dirt over the side until finally all that was left in the "V" formed by the side and bottom of the pan was a black residue. If lucky, he might find a nugget in this black sand; but the miner felt fortunate if he only found "colors" in the pan. These were small particles of gold about the size of a pinhead which could be picked out with forceps. The flour gold could be separated from the residue by adding a bit of mercury which has an affinity for gold. The mercury was then separated from the gold by evaporation in a closed container. The gold pan was the most primitive device for recovering gold, but in the hands of an experienced miner it was one of the best. The major disadvantage of the pan was the limited amount of soil and gravel which could be worked.

A miner's ingenuity and a few pieces of scrap wood and metal could create such devices as the rocker, the Long Tom, and the sluice box. The rocker, which was somewhat like a child's cradle, had holes bored in it at one end near the bottom. At the other end was a riddle or a tray that was punched full of holes. The operator shoveled dirt into the tray, poured water on top, and rocked the device back and forth. The heavy gold would settle in cleats at the bottom of the rocker as the water washed the lighter materials through. The Long Tom was a wooden trough, elevated at the narrower end where water entered, and with a riddle at the wider downhill end to catch the gold washed from the dirt. The sluice box was also a wooden trough about a foot wide and six to ten inches deep. But the sluice box was quite long, often over a hundred feet in length. Removable frames or riffles or cleats were placed the length of the sluice box. Operation of the Long Tom, and especially of the sluice box, necessitated the cooperation of a number of miners. Great amounts of water were needed to operate both devices, and ditches or flumes were constructed to carry the water, sometimes for miles. A sluice box would keep many men busy shoveling in the dirt to be washed.

In California, distinction was made between wet diggings, where all the gold was procured through washing, and dry diggings. In these dry diggings, which were usually located in ravines, the surface rocks and earth were removed exposing little crevices and holes. These "pockets" usually contained free gold which could be dug out with a knife or sharp object.

Every prospector dreamed of such an occurrence as was described by one successful group of gold-seekers:

We had packed on the back of one of our mules
a sufficient number of boards . . . to construct a
machine, and the morning after our arrival placed
two of our party at work for this purpose, while
the rest of us were to dig; and taking our pans,
crowbars, and picks, we commenced operations.
Our first attempt was to search around the base of
a lofty boulder, which weighed probably some
twenty tons, in hopes of finding a crevice in the
rock on which it rested, in which a deposit of gold
might have been made; nor were we unsuccessful.
Around the base of the rock was a filling up of
gravel and clay, which we removed with much
labour, when our eyes were gladdened with the
sight of gold strewn all over its surface, and inter-
mixed with a blackish sand. This we gathered up
and washed in our pans, and ere night four of us
had dug and washed twenty-six ounces of gold,
being about four hundred and sixteen dollars.[8]

It has been stated that men never worked so hard in all
their lives to get rich without working. The tales of riches
to be picked off the ground gave way to the hard reality that
mining was backbreaking work with no assurance of even
making expenses. But the miner remained optimistic and
listened eagerly to every new rumor of a big strike near
Loafer Hill, Slapjack Bar; Chicken-thief Flat; Git-up-and-
Git; Rat-trap Slide; Sweet Revenge; Shirt-tail Canon; You
Bet; or Gouge Eye. The prospectors, like the mountain men,
seemed to be always traveling—traveling in search of a new
Eldorado.

An isolated ravine in the midst of a wilderness could be
transformed overnight into a booming mining camp. The
letters of Dame Shirley (Louise Amelia Knapp Smith Clappe)
to her sister Molly, in "the States," provide some of the
finest accounts of life in the mining camps. Dame Shirley
related the establishment of Rich Bar, the mining town in
which her husband was a physician.

[8] Bingham, *California Gold*, p. 20.

On arriving at Rich Bar a [group of miners] camped there, but many went a few miles further down the river. The next morning two men turned over a large stone, beneath which they found quite a sizable piece of gold. They washed a small pan-full of the dirt, and obtained from it two hundred and fifty-six dollars. Encouraged by this success, they commenced staking off the legal amount of ground allowed to each person for mining pur-poses; and, the remainder of the party having descended the hill, before night the entire bar was "claimed". In a fortnight from that time, the two men who found the first bit of gold had each taken out six thousand dollars. Two others took out thirty-three pounds of gold in eight hours; which is the best day's work that has been done on this branch of the river; the largest amount ever taken from one panful of dirt was fifteen hundred dollars. In little more than a week after its discovery, five hundred men had settled upon the bar for the summer.—Such is the wonderful alacrity with which a mining town is built.[9]

Mining Towns

Food, shelter, and clothing of the miners in the usual mining town were as simple, and even crude, as the miner was willing to tolerate. There wasn't time for such non-essentials, especially in the first few months when prospects of making a paying strike were good. In the winter of 1848, outbreaks of "land scurvy" were widespread. Perhaps as many as one-half of the miners in northern California ex-perienced the disease which resulted from a diet of salt meat almost entirely. Fresh vegetables were difficult to obtain and were too costly for most of the miners. Unaccustomed to living constantly exposed to the elements, and with insuf-ficient clothing, many of the miners being in poor physical condition did not survive the disease.

[9] *Ibid.*, p. 94.

Transportation to many of the mining camps was difficult. Primitive roads and long distances contributed to the high prices at the mines. Flour cost one dollar per pound, molasses four dollars per gallon, sugar a dollar per pound, and tobacco sold at two dollars per pound. In one recorded instance two miners, on their way to a sawmill, were unable to obtain a meal and were obliged to purchase the ingredients for their breakfast.

One box of sardines	$16.00
One pound of hard bread	2.00
One pound of butter	6.00
A half-pound of cheese	3.00
Two bottles of ale	16.00
Total	$43.00 [10]

One party of four, planning for six months of prospecting, purchased the following items:

3 yoke of oxen at $75 per yoke	$225.00
1 wagon	85.00
1 tent and poles—the latter ironed	15.00
1 Dutch oven, for baking bread	1.25
1 wooden bucket	.25
4 steel picks, with handles	9.50
4 steel shovels, Ames' make	6.00
5 gold pans, largest size	4.00
Sheet iron for Long Tom	.75
Pair of gold scales	2.00
3 gallons of Brandy	12.00
8 pounds of gunpowder	3.20
25 pounds of lead	2.50
10 pounds of shot	1.00
2000 gun caps	1.20
10 yards drilling, for sluice	1.25 [11]

[10] *Ibid.*, p. 24.
[11] From *The First Hundred Years* (p. 14) by Robert L. Perkin. (© 1959 by the Denver Publishing Co. By permission of Doubleday and Co., Inc.)

The merchants, the traders, and the transporters of provisions, profited more from the miners' labor than did the miners.

"The typical camp of the golden prime of '49 was flush, lively, reckless, flourishing, and vigorous," wrote Charles Howard Shinn.

> Saloons and gambling-houses abounded; buildings and whole streets grew up like mushrooms, almost in a night. Every man carried a buckskin bag of gold-dust, and it was received as currency at a dollar a pinch. Every one went armed, and felt fully able to protect himself. A stormy life ebbed and flowed through the town. In the camp, gathered as of one household, under no law but that of their own making, were men from North, South, East, and West, and from nearly every country of Europe, Asia, South America. They mined, traded, gambled, fought, discussed camp affairs; they paid fifty cents a drink for their whiskey, and fifty dollars a barrel for their flour, and thirty dollars apiece for butcher-knives with which to pick gold from the rock crevices.[12]

The first dwellings of the miners were tents which had been erected, taken down, and moved so many times that they were quite well worn. The tent camps gave way to more permanent dwellings; brush and pole houses which were dug partially back into a hillside and provided with a dirt roof were cool in the summer and warm in the winter. Log cabins replaced the ruder habitations, especially after a miner endured an often mud-dripping roof which had been thoroughly soaked by a long rain. Until sawed lumber became available at prices the miner could afford, he would be content with a hard-packed earthen or clay floor.

Some cabins were furnished with chairs and tables formed of split poles from the forest with the bark still on them. The cabin floor was often partially covered with a bearskin

[12] Shinn, *op. cit.*, p. 147.

or raw hides. The miner's bed was usually a wooden platform fastened to the log wall and covered with hay. There was the total absence of timber in the immediate area. It had been taken for cabins, firewood, sluice boxes, and where lode mining was practiced, much of the timber was used in shoring up mine tunnels.

The very new mining towns, particularly those of 1848, were usually quite law-abiding. The apparent abundance of gold inspired the inhabitant to long hours of feverish activity with their washing pans, Long Toms, and sluice boxes. There was little time for planning ahead, little time for formulating rules, little time for diversions—which might include washing clothes, observing the Sabbath, or reading a scarce newspaper or book.

In these early camps, crime was almost unknown. It was easier for a man to wash gold than to steal it. Strangers were welcomed as equals. A man could go into another miner's cabin, help himself to a slice of bacon or cook a meal, roll up in a blanket and go to sleep with the knowledge that he would be welcomed by the returning owner.

But as the mining towns grew, the original bonds of fellowship disappeared. All elements of society were attracted to the gold-fields, lured by reports that miners were making between $20 and $30 a day. Men who were making $1 a day in the East found the temptation to go West irresistible. But many swindlers, bandits, and gamblers were also attracted by the free-spending of miners who were accustomed to paying $100 for a pair of boots and who thought little of gambling away nearly everything they earned.

Frank Marryat recorded in *Mountains and Molehills* his recollections of California mining towns in the early 1850's. He described the average saloon as dazzling to the eye by the brilliancy of chandeliers and mirrors.

> The roof, rich with giltwork, is supported by pillars of glass; and the walls are hung with French paintings of great merit . . . . Green tables are

> scattered over the room, at each of which sit two "monte" dealers surrounded by a betting crowd. The centres of the tables are covered with gold ounces and rich specimens from the diggings, and these heaps accumulate very rapidly in the course of the evening . . . the dealer is intently watched by a hundred eyes, whose owners, in revenge for having lost, would gladly detect a cheat, and fall upon him and tear him to pieces . . . .[13]

Though gambling was a major form of entertainment in the mining towns, the miners enjoyed singing and dancing, fiddle-playing, cockfights, fights between a bear and a bull, and the occasional visits of traveling entertainers.

Lawlessness in a mining camp, which was the nucleus of a general mining district, was discouraged by the process of referring the offender to the judgment of the majority. The often-quoted statement, "We needed no law until the lawyers came," reflected the frontier desire for prompt justice unhampered by legal technicalities and delays. The usual punishments for wrongdoers, thieves, and other undesirables took the forms of whippings, banishment from the district, or fines. If an offending miner was fined, it was customary to permit retention of his basic tools of mining, usually to the value of about $20.

Excessive drinking and gambling all too often indicated a general absence of social restraint in many mining communities. The historian Ray Allen Billington observed in his study of the California Gold Rush that the absence of social pressures also inspired a completely undemocratic nativism:

> Mexicans, Chinese, and Indians were shamefully abused by the "Yankee" majority, under the theory that "coloured men were not privileged to work in a country intended only for American citizens". In nearly all camps Mexicans were driven from their claims by mobs, Chinese were

[13] Bingham, *op. cit.*, p. 74.

heavily taxed or forced to work mines abandoned by others, and Indians mercilessly slaughtered. That Americans could be converted into such heartless nativists was indicative of the corrosive effect of the environment.[14]

ISHI

On the morning of August 29, 1911, a wild Indian was found on the outskirts of Oroville, California. He could not understand a word of English. Hunger had driven him from his home in the hills. Not knowing what else to do, the sheriff put him in jail for safe keeping. Fortunately, a story in the local paper came to the attention of anthropologists at the University of California. One of them immediately went to see the Indian.

In the jail, the anthropologist sat beside him on a wooden bench and hopefully began reading off a list of Indian words. Almost at the end of the list, he read "swini," which is the Yahi word meaning white pine. The Indian's face brightened. In his excitement, he pounded on the pine bench. This was a word he knew. A way had been found for the two men to talk together.

The Indian asked his visitor, "I ne ma Yahi?" That means: "Are you a Yahi?" The anthropogist nodded his head. He knew the Indian really was asking, "Are you my friend?"

True to his tribal custom, this Indian never spoke his true name. In the future he was to be known as Ishi. That is the Yahi word meaning man.

Ishi had literally stumbled from a stone age life into the twentieth century. He was the last wild Indian in America.

He went with his new friend to live in the San Francisco Museum. There his remarkable story unfolded. His tribe, the strong and proud Yahi, living in northern California, had been nearly

[14] Billington, *The Far Western Frontier,* p. 238.

wiped out by the white men who poured in with the gold rush. At last, only Ishi, his elderly mother, his sister, and an uncle were left. In spite of the increasing number of settlers, this small band kept its tribal life and lived in strict hiding.

In one tragedy after another, the other members of the family died, and for two years Ishi lived alone—until fate brought him into civilization.

Ishi lived in the museum until his death. He was beloved by all who worked there. Besides serving as a caretaker of the museum, he helped the anthropologists record the entire language of his people. He helped map the Yahi country as he had lived in it. A master craftsman, he turned out enough fine bows and arrows and arrowheads and other artifacts to set up a Yahi collection in the museum.

Of this man who distinguished himself in two worlds, T. T. Waterman, curator of the museum, said: "To know him was a rare personal privilege, . . . I feel myself that in many ways he was perhaps the most remarkable personality of his century." [15]

In the absence of established agencies of law enforcement, so-called "vigilance committees" were formed whose membership might, or might not, have represented the law-abiding residents of a mining town. The purpose of such organizations was to bring order to a district threatened by lawless elements. These committees would often apprehend a suspected enemy of society, determine the punishment, and carry out the sentence. Two letters of Dame Shirley reflect a change in attitude toward the merit of vigilance committees:

From our Log Cabin, Indian Bar
December 15, 1851

. . . The Vigilance Committee, [of San Francisco] had become absolutely necessary for the protec-

[15] Caughey, Franklin & May, *Land of the Free,* Vol. 2, p. 108.

tion of society. It was composed of the best and wisest men in the city. They used their powers with a moderation unexampled in history, and they laid it down with a calm and quiet readiness which was absolutely sublime, when they found that legal justice had again resumed that course of stern, unflinching duty which should always be its characteristic. They took ample time for a thorough investigation of all the circumstances relating to the criminals who fell into their hands; and in *no* case have they hung a man, who had not been proved beyond the shadow of a doubt, to have committed at least *one* robbery in which life had been endangered, if not absolutely taken . . .[16]

Eight months later, Dame Shirley wrote to her sister in the East informing her of the establishment of a vigilance committee in the mining camp in which she resided.

> From our Log Cabin, Indian Bar
> August 4, 1852

. . . The state of society here has never been so bad as since the appointment of a Committee of Vigilance. The rowdies have formed themselves into a company called the "Moguls," and they parade the streets all night, howling, shouting, breaking into houses, taking wearied miners out of their beds and throwing them into the river, and in short, "murdering sleep," in the most remorseless manner. Nearly every night they build bonfires fearfully near some rag shanty, thus endangering the lives . . . of the whole community. They retire about five o'clock in the morning; previously to this blessed event posting notices to that effect, and that they will throw any one who may disturb them into the river. I am nearly worn out for want of rest, for truly they "make night hideous" with their fearful uproar.[17]

[16] Bingham, *op. cit.,* p. 102.
[17] Hine and Bingham, *The Frontier Experience,* p. 230.

In July 1849, delegates from all over California met to write a state constitution. In late 1849, the people of California applied for statehood which Congress approved the next year. Most of the mining camps declined into ghost towns after the placers or lodes had been worked out. A few of the mining towns attained permanence. Local government was instituted, schools established, literary societies formed, newspapers published, and theaters or opera houses were constructed. Perhaps indicative of the quality of the literary societies of many mining towns was Frank Marrayat's observation that literary societies were established by profane illiterates who were as unfamiliar with books as with morality. One "literary" society provided entertainment for members by spinning a hat to see who would pay for drinks.

The formation of mining districts and the drafting of mining codes were better indications of growing social and legal stability in the western mining regions.

Mining Government

During the first year of the California gold rush, crimes were rare. The seeming abundance of rich placers and relatively few numbers of miners in the Sierras made the establishment of rules and regulations unnecessary. Many of the miners from Oregon had organized small mining companies before setting out for the gold-fields. The members of such companies would agree to abide by certain rules. One small mining company drew up the following set of rules:

(1) That we shall bear an equal share in all expenses.

(2) That no man shall be allowed to leave the company without general consent till we reach the mines.

(3) That any one leaving with our consent shall have back his original investment.

(4) That we work together in the mines, and use our tools in common.

(5) That each man shall retain all the gold he finds, but must contribute an equal portion of our daily expenses.

(6) That we stand by each other.

(7) That each man shall in turn cook, and do his share of the drudgery.

(8) That any one guilty of stealing shall be expelled from tent and claim, with such other punishment as a majority of our company decide upon.

(9) That no sick comrade be abandoned.[18]

These small companies of miners considered no other rule beyond that of the majority of its own members. Such was the first government in many of the mining camps.

No attempts were made to formulate rules in the remainder of the mining camps until a need for them became apparent —and no sooner.

> When we come back to dinner, Bill an' I, two strange fellers was at work in our claim. We sat down on the bank, an' told them there was plenty of good gravel, jest as good, a mile down the river, an' that was our diggin's. They didn't stir, so one of us went an' asked Cap'n Bob Porter, the best an' quietest man in camp, to come up; an' we all had a drink outen the cap'n's flask, an' then we talked it over, he bein' spokesman. Pretty soon they said it warn't no use making a row, an' went off very friendly.[19]

Such informal agreements soon became impractical. The miners began to hold meetings in order to draw up definite rules and regulations pertaining to the size, ownership, and working of the claims. These miners' meetings were the first

[18] Shinn, *op. cit.*, p. 113.
[19] *Ibid.*, p. 174.

attempts at self-government in the frontier gold camps. There was no authority to which a miner could appeal beyond the majority of those in attendance at such a miners' meeting.

Decisions involving civil complaints were made by miners in attendance at a miners' "court." Such decisions were reached by the process of majority opinion. In all too many decisions, however, it was charged that the opinion of the court had been swayed. Bribing of the miners in attendance by providing them with whiskey influenced more than one court. Criminals were also tried and punished by miners' courts. Lacking jails and jailers, the courts were limited to three penalties: whipping, banishment, and death.

A miners' court could be assembled in minutes by dispatching a messenger through the diggings. If the mining camp was large, a jury might be appointed to hear the case and render a verdict, but more often the jury consisted of the miners in attendance. A miners' court might reach a verdict and carry out the punishment all within an hour's time, as was once the case on which a cold-blooded murder was witnessed by twelve miners. In another instance, a miners' court took four days to hear testimony and reach a verdict.

As the process of self-government became well established in the mining camps, written bodies of law were formulated to provide organized government. These written bodies of law, or constitutions, derived their authority from the consent of the miners. A constitution was drawn up after an assembly of miners within a general area formed a mining district. Each organized district provided four essentials: (1) The name of the district; (2) the boundaries of the district; (3) the officers who were to execute the laws of a district; (4) laws to regulate the size and ownership of mining claims.

The boundaries of a mining district were of two general types: Using the original discovery claim as its center, a district could have boundaries which formed a rectangular area. The boundaries of a district might follow the summit of a ridge which separated two gulches, or perhaps just a stream bed. Whichever the case, it was the intention of the mining district to establish very definite boundaries. The size of a district could depend upon the extent of the gold deposits or the type of deposits. The mining districts of Colorado, the Black Hills, Montana, and Idaho were usually smaller than those of California because the gold was more concentrated in lode deposits instead of placers.

The officers of a mining district, with some variations, would include a president, a recorder, and a sheriff. In California, the president was often designated the *alcalde*. The alcalde was the head man of those California villages in which Spanish culture predominated. The president who presided at the miners' meetings was judge of the miners' courts, and usually had the authority to settle minor disputes within the district.

The recorder, or secretary, kept records of claims filed within the district, claims transferred, and other written documents on the payment of a fee. Portions of the fees collected constituted the recorder's pay. His job also included taking minutes at the miners' meetings.

The sheriff was charged with preserving the peace, which in some districts was a very hazardous occupation. The sheriff received much of his pay through serving writs and a percentage of the proceeds on sheriff's sales of properties on which there were judgments.

The officers were elected at miners' meetings after publicly declaring themselves to be nominees. Many districts were lenient in voter requirements, establishing a minimum age of sixteen years and residence in the district for ten days. Many districts, especially those in the Rocky Mountain regions, allowed women to hold mining claims and these districts may have allowed women to vote.

In most mining districts, anyone over sixteen years of age could hold a mining claim. To make a legal claim, the discoverer would first locate it by staking the claim at each end and mark the name of the claim, the date and direction as well as the dimensions of the claim, and his own name. Then, within ten days the discoverer had to file his location with the district recorder. Thirty days was the amount of time allowed to prove the claim. If it was a lode claim, the discoverer was required to expose the lode within the thirty days. The original discoverer was also allowed one additional claim before others were allowed to file on the lode.

When a miner recorded his claim, a certificate of title was given him as the owner by the district recorder or president. Most mining districts required a certain amount of work to be done on a claim. If a claim was not worked within a stipulated amount of time, the claim was declared vacant and another miner could file upon it.

Many Forty-Niners participated in later gold rushes in other regions of the West. They brought with them experience in mining techniques and the techniques of self-government which were learned in those early mining camps. These experienced miners helped to make the constitutions of later mining districts so well formulated that their provisions were recognized as legal by the territorial and state governments which followed.

Much of California's gold was found in placer deposits. These types of claims came to be known as gulch claims in the Rocky Mountain mining districts, since the gold was found loose in gulches or stream beds. A gulch claim usually extended from bank to bank for about one hundred feet up and down the gulch. More often, in the Rocky Mountains, a miner would make a mountain or a lode claim. These claims were generally one hundred feet long and fifty feet wide, twenty-five feet on each side of the lode or vein.

Water was the life blood of mining. Water was necessary in washing placer gold and in the crushing and separating processes of lode gold. Claims to a distance of a running stream were called "water claims." Because room was needed to build and operate sluice boxes, rockers and Long Toms, a portion of the adjoining land was also included in a water claim. If a miner wished to build a stamp mill alongside a stream in order to utilize the water power in operating the stamps, he would make a mill site claim. This type of claim specified that the size of the claim was determined by the distance up and down the stream necessary to give sufficient head to a dam. In most cases, the dam had to raise the water fourteen feet which was enough fall to turn a mill wheel.

Claims to parcels of land, not in gulches, containing loose gold were called patch diggings claims and were 100 feet square. Many a greenhorn was sold a worthless claim of this type which had been "salted."

There were additional types of mining claims, and as mining became more complex, particularly hard-rock mining, the provisions of these claims became more complex. In addition to mineral claims were timber claims, ranch claims, and cabin claims.

Although miners tended to regard lawyers with suspicion and even unfriendliness, it was obvious that a good many of the constitutions of later mining districts were drawn up by legally trained individuals.

After the first miners had taken that gold which was relatively easy to secure, the mining industry began to require expensive machinery for processing the ores. A large amount of capital was required to build mills, dig tunnels and shafts, and to hire the men who worked the mines. Eventually, the prospector gave way to the industrialist. The Forty-Niner who did not return to the East, or follow rumors of big strikes in Nevada, or Colorado, or Dakota Territory, went back to what he knew best—farming. And what had, for a short time, been the rip-roaring boom town of Red Dog Camp, or Mad Mule Gulch, or Murderer's Bar, existed only as another ghost town.

"The saddest of all possible sights in the old mining region," observed one of the pioneers:

> is where there are not even half a dozen miners
> to keep each other company, but where, solitary
> and in desolation, the last miner clings to his
> former haunts. He cooks his lonesome meals in

the wrecked and rotting hotel where a quarter of a century before, then young, gay, prosperous, and in his prime, he had tossed the reins of his livery-team to the . . . servant, and played billiards with the "boys", and passed the hat for a collection to build the first church.[20]

But the miner's frontier also provided its lessons in democracy:

As we have seen, there were times in almost every camp when the rowdy element came near ruling, and only the powerful and hereditary organizing instincts of the Americans present ever brought order out of the chaos . . . . Side by side in the same gulch, working in claims of eight paces square, were, perhaps, fishermen from Cape Ann, loggers from Penobscot, farmers from the Genesee Valley, physicians from the prairies of Iowa, lawyers from Maryland and Louisiana, college-graduates from Yale, Harvard, and the University of Virginia. From so variously mingled elements, came that terribly exacting mining-camp society, which tested with pitiless and unerring tests each man's individual manhood, discovering his intrinsic worth or weakness with almost superhuman precision, until at last the ablest and best men became leaders.[21]

[20] Shinn, *op. cit.*, pp. 146–6.
[21] *Ibid.*, pp. 148–9.

Bibliography

Angle, Paul M.	*The American Reader* Rand McNally, New York, N.Y.	1958 ed.
Billington, Ray Allen	*The Far Western Frontier* Harper & Row, New York, N.Y.	1956 ed.
Bingham, Edwin R.	*California Gold* D. C. Heath, Boston, Mass.	1959 ed.
Dick, Everett	*Vanguards of the Frontier* University of Nebraska Press, Lincoln, Neb.	1941 ed.
Fritz, Percy S.	*Colorado, The Centennial State* Prentice-Hall, New York, N.Y.	1941 ed.
Hafen, Leroy R. and Ann W.	*Journals of Forty-niners* Arthur H. Clark Co., Glendale, Calif.	1954 ed.
Hine, Robert V. and Bingham, Edwin R.	*The Frontier Experience* Wadsworth Publishing Co., Belmont, Calif.	1963 ed.
Marryat, Francis Samuel	*Mountains and Molehills* Lippincott, New York, N.Y.	1962 ed.
Paul, Rodman Wilson	*Mining Frontiers of the Far West* Holt, Rinehart, Winston, New York, N.Y.	1963 ed.
Peters, Harry T.	*California on Stone* Doubleday, Garden City, N.Y.	1935 ed.
Potter, David M.	*Trail to California* Yale University Press, New Haven, Conn.	1945 ed.
Shinn, Charles Howard	*Mining Camps, A Study in Ameri- can Frontier Government* Harper & Row, New York, N.Y.	1965 ed.

5 | The Cattlemen

In discussing the rancher's frontier, Frederick Jackson Turner recognized its two most significant aspects—the long drive from Texas to the Kansas railroad towns or the northern ranges, and the evolution of large ranches on the Great Plains. He was aware also of the remoteness of these Great Plains.

> . . . Travelers of the eighteenth century found the "cowpens" among the canebrakes and peavine pastures of the South, and the "cow drivers" took their droves to Charleston, Philadelphia, and New York. Travelers at the close of the War of 1812 met droves of more than a thousand cattle and swine from the interior of Ohio going to Pennsyl-

vania to fatten for the Philadelphia market. The ranges of the Great Plains, with ranch and cowboy and nomadic life, are things of yesterday and of to-day. The experience of the Carolina cowpens guided the ranchers of Texas. One element favoring the rapid extension of the rancher's frontier is the fact that in a remote country lacking transportation facilities the product must be in small bulk, or must be able to transport itself, and the cattle raiser could easily drive his product to market. The effect of these great ranches on the subsequent agrarian history of the localities in which they existed should be studied.[1]

But even as he spoke, the range cattle industry was declining and, like the frontier itself, would soon cease to exist. By 1905 the great range herds had disappeared. Owen Wister's classic, *The Virginian,* was published in that year, beginning the process of romanticizing the cowboy and the Great Plains—America's last frontier.

Romanticizing the cowboy is best described by a Colorado rancher who, twenty-five years after first reading Wister's book, wrote the author that:

> Reading them chapters fetched me west, aheading straight for Wyoming which I never reached, altho I've been in every other western state in all these years. . . . No I never saw Wyoming or saw the Wind River Country. I did see the Ranch in Idaho where the hanging took place. Hunted sage chickens there, meby not the real ranch but it had the cottonwoods and the smell of sage in the rain. Anyway it fitted the frame of the picture you made of it. I've got a feeling low down in my heart that I shouldn't ever go to your Wyoming now. It might not be as perfect as you fixed it in your books. Perhaps I'm illusioned about that

[1] Turner, *Significance, op. cit.,* pp. 38–9.

country and I wouldn't want it to be different
than it is in my mind.[2]

The Wyoming of Wister's novel was but a part of the
Great Plains, a vast area west of the 98th meridian to the
Rocky Mountains—level, treeless, semi-arid, an environment
totally different from any previous frontier. The Great Plains
were conquered only after the Industrial Revolution provided
the tools in the form of windmills and barbed wire. Our
interest, as expressed by Walter Prescott Webb, is:

> . . . in the process by which man in relation to
> his environment evolved around cattle the institu-
> tion of ranching. In this evolution the Plains
> worked their will, and man conformed. The Plains
> put men on horseback and taught them to work
> in that way . . . . In the end the cattle kingdom
> occupied practically the whole Great Plains envi-
> ronment; it was the most natural economic and
> social order that the white man had yet developed
> in his experiment with the Great Plains.[3]

Although the cattle kingdom had its beginnings in Texas
roughly about 1840, it was not until after the Civil War that
the range cattle industry assumed its distinctive aspects of
trail drives and large ranches. The real era of the rancher's
frontier begins with the first drive of Texas longhorns across
the Red River to northern markets in 1866 and ends with the
loss of 85 per cent of the range cattle in the blizzards of
1885–86.

What were the characteristics of the rancher's frontier?
How did this frontier differ from other frontiers? What intellectual traits can be associated with the cattlemen? An understanding of this period of 1855–1885 on the Great Plains

[2] Lambert, "A Cowboy Writes to Owen Wister," Vol. II, No. 4, 1965,
pp. 33–6. (Permission of *The American West* Magazine.)
[3] Webb, *op. cit.*, p. 226.

and a study of the rancher and cowboy may provide some answers.

The Cowboy

The cowboy's occupation was the most natural of the American West. It was natural because it took the Great Plains as they were—grasslands—and used them in their natural state. This closeness to nature was one of the characteristics of the cowboy.

> Perhaps the strength and originality in his speech are due to the solitude, the nearness of the stars, the bigness of the country, and the far horizons—all of which give him a chance to think clearly and go into the depths of his own mind . . . . Unlettered men rely greatly upon comparisons to natural objects with which they are familiar to express their ideas and feelings.[4]

Such was the observation of Ramon Adams, himself a cowboy and author of *Western Words,* perhaps the most complete compilation of terms and words used by the cowboy. Adams describes the cowboy as:

> . . . a man who followed the cows. A generation ago the East knew him as a bloody demon of disaster, reckless and rowdy, weighted down with weapons, and ever ready to use them. Today he is known as the hero of a wild west story, as the eternally hard-riding movie actor, as the "guitar pickin'" yodeler, or the gayly bedecked rodeo follower.
> The West, who knows him best, knows that he has always been "just a plain, everyday bow-legged

[4] From *Western Words* (p. viii) by Ramon F. Adams. (© 1944 by the University of Oklahoma Press.)

human," carefree and courageous, fun-loving and
loyal, uncomplaining and doing his best to live up
to a tradition of which he is proud.[5]

The cowboy was courageous. Isolated from other people,
removed from law and order, customs and society, he had to
be courageous. Walter Prescott Webb wrote that:

> Courage became a fundamental and essential at-
> tribute in the [cowboy] . . . . The germ of courage
> had to be in him; but this germ being given, the
> life that he led developed it to a high degree.
> Where men are . . . in constant danger or even po-
> tential danger, they will not tolerate the coward.[6]

Courage alone did not guarantee survival, or even success as
a cowboy; self-reliance and willingness to drop old methods
and adopt new ones better fitted to his Great Plains environment were also characteristics of the cattleman.

That he was fun-loving hardly needs explanation. Long
periods of routine, hard work, isolation and boredom were
compensated for by a few nights in town which gave the
cowboy a reputation of being rowdy, perhaps lawless, and
most certainly a spendthrift with his pay of thirty to sixty
dollars a month. But such a reputation was acquired by gen-
eralizing upon these relatively brief instances in which he was
observed by many of the town's citizens. In her book, *The
Cattlemen,* Mari Sandoz wrote of the hardworking cowhand:

> . . . often rowdy when he hit town, spurring his
> horse and popping his pistol, to scatter the anklers,
> the people afoot, send them fleeing through the
> dusty street like a settler's hens before the hawk's
> approach. He was still sometimes a thief or a

[5] Pp. 41–42 (© 1944 by the University of Oklahoma Press.)
[6] Webb, *op. cit.,* p. 245.

116

killer, as his boss might very well be, but any
man who wasn't a worker, hardy, tough, and full
of sand, wouldn't stick with the cow business long
enough to pay for his saddle.[7]

The average cowboy was young. Anyone over thirty years
of age on a ranch or a trail drive was considered an "old
man." He was often an individual looking for excitement—
or fleeing from trouble—and as a result, he was not highly
educated. This may account for so few accounts of the cowboy's life written *by* a cowboy during the period of the open
range and height of the cattleman's frontier. One such account does exist, however; and *The Log of a Cowboy* by
Andy Adams is the most authentic piece of literature ever
written about the cowboy.

The form of humor employed by a cowboy on a ranch or
during a trail drive differed greatly from that observed by
the "paper-collar Comanches" of the cowtowns, as the cowboy referred to the merchants. Adams related one instance
in which the foreman of a trail drive appointed one of his
cowboys, Joe Stallings, to be *segundo* in his absence. Joe good
naturedly took advantage of the situation by assigning the
other men to the cook's duties including standing his night
guard, this in return for the cook's promise to provide jam
and jelly for the next Sunday. Upon returning from night
guard, one of the imposed-upon cowboys:

> . . . intentionally walked across Stalling's bed,
> and catching his spur in the tarpaulin, fell heavily
> across our *segundo*.
> "Excuse me," said John [the cowboy returning
> from night guard,] rising, "but I was just nosing
> around looking for the foreman. Oh, it's you, is
> it? I just wanted to ask if 4.30 wouldn't be plenty
> early to build up the fire. Wood's a little scarce,
> but I'll burn the prairies if you say so. That's all

[7] P. 100. (© 1958 Hasting House.)

I wanted to know; you may lay down now and go to sleep." [8]

Concerning the cowboy's characteristic of loyalty, J. Frank Dobie, foremost authority on the American Southwest, observed that: "Loyalty is more pronounced, it seems to me, in individuals not ambitious for themselves than in those who are. It is marked in certain hirelings without hope or intention of rising in the economic scale to be employers." Dobie illustrated the cowboy's loyalty with the following story in his book, *Cow People:*

> In 1882, Joe Erricson, a native of Sweden, nineteen years old, hired himself to help fence the far-spread S M S ranches in west Texas. In time he became range boss over seventy-five cowboys, twenty-five thousand cattle and five hundred saddle horses. Then he married a lady who found ranch life far from attractive. He quit the land of grass and silences and moved with her to pavement and noises. Six months later he showed up in the office of A. J. Swenson, part owner and manager of the S M S's. "Andrew," he announced, "I'm lonesome." "Lonesome, Joe. For what?" "For the ranch. If you have a place for me, I'm coming back." A. J. Swenson put him in charge of the Spur Ranch of about half a million acres. There he lived and worked the remainder of his life. When he died in 1931 he had ridden S M S horses for nearly fifty years.
>
> In August of that year he was confined to the house that was his home, but was still keeping up with ranch affairs. One morning he called a man in and told him to hitch his pair of bays to the buggy and drive him to where a herd of S M S cattle was being worked, a few miles away. When they arrived at the edge of the roundup grounds,

[8] From *The Log of a Cowboy* (pp. 234–5) by Andy Adams, © 1903. (By permission of the University of Nebraska Press.)

he gave the driver a sign to stop. The buggy top was down. He rose to his feet, one hand on the dashboard, and stood in silence gazing at the cattle and the riders. Then he turned his head as if to look again at the Caprock in the hazy distance. Without a word he sank to the seat from which he had risen. He was dead.

Joe Erricson was loyal to the Swensons, loyal to his work, loyal to the S M S tradition. His loyalties seemed to depend upon following the life inside himself, the only kind of life he got satisfaction from—ranch life. He had to be true to himself.[9]

The cowboy was as uncomplaining as he was loyal. "Kickin' never gets you nowhere 'less you're a mule." The cowboy preferred to be optimistic about any situation no matter how bad it might appear. He seldom complained but chose to "swallow his trouble with his food."

His reluctance to exhibit any show of sentiment contrasted with his vanity particularly as demonstrated in his equipment and his clothing. His favorite recreation was swapping stories around a campfire, especially in the evenings during a long drive. The stories usually related to the superiority of some favored "hoss" or in contemplating a race between two highly esteemed horses. But occasionally the stories related to "the States," or home; and in attempting to put on a rough exterior, he would explain away a sentiment-induced tear with the statement that, "The smoke of your camp-fire got into my eyes."

The cowboy's fondness for ornate equipment is illustrated in the saying, "a forty-dollar saddle on a ten-dollar hoss." Though his equipment and clothing were often ornate and even exaggerated at times, they were practical. A big, broad-brimmed hat served as an umbrella protecting the wearer from sun and weather. A neckerchief drawn over the face pro-

[9] Dobie, *Cow People,* pp. 216–7. (© 1964 by J. Frank Dobie. By permission of Little, Brown and Co.)

tected him from dust, and chaps or chaparejos protected his legs while riding through brush. High-heeled boots made riding easier and protected the ankles from constant chafing. And as his spurs were an occupational necessity, so too were they a social necessity when on foot—even if he were at a dance!

The term cowboy originated in the southern Appalachian Mountains of eastern United States about the time of the American Revolution; but the influence of the East ends with the contribution of the term cowboy for the Western herdsman. Many authorities on the American West prefer the use of two terms in referring to the cattlemen of the West—cowboy for those men who worked cattle east of the Rocky Mountains and *vaquero* for those whose territory lay west of the Rockies. Americans anglicized this latter term to "buckaroo." But whether these cowboys, vaqueros, or buckaroos worked in Texas, Montana, or California, they faced much the same difficulties and dangers. Cowboys were Mexicans, Indians, Anglos, and Negroes. Just after the Civil War, over 5,000 Negroes were herding cattle in the West.

Of the American Negro as cowboys, Philip Durham and Everett L. Jones, in their book, *The Negro Cowboys,* observed that:

> Now they are forgotten, but once they rode all the trails, driving millions of cattle before them. Some died in stampedes, some froze to death, some drowned. Some were too slow with guns, some too fast. But most of them lived through the long drives to Abilene, to Dodge City, to Ogallala. And many of them drove on to the farthest reaches of the northern range, to the Dakotas, Wyoming and Montana.
>
> They numbered thousands, among them many of the best riders, ropers and wranglers. They hunted wild horses and wolves, and a few of them hunted men. Some were villains, some were heroes. Some were called offensive names, and others were given

almost equally offensive compliments. But even
when one of them was praised as "the whitest man
I've ever known," he was not white.[10]

An average trail drive numbering some 2,500 head of cattle
would be handled by twelve to fifteen cowhands; and of this
number, at least two or three drovers were usually Negro and
often the cook as well.

The Drover

The cattle that the cowboys herded, the horses that they
rode, much of the equipment that they used, and a large proportion of the language and terminology that they employed
were Spanish in their origin. Coronado's expedition to the
Southwest in 1540 brought the first cattle and horses to North
America. And during the next two and a half centuries, the
establishment of Spanish missions and ranches in northern
New Mexico, west Texas, southern Arizona, and the Pacific
coast of California provided the nucleus of wild herds of
longhorns and mustangs. Frank Dobie, in his book *The Longhorns,* states that:

> The Longhorn was, . . . basically Spanish. Yet,
> when he entered upon the epoch of his continent-
> marking history, he was as Texan as his counter-
> part, the Texas cowboy. *Cavalier* means "horse-
> man." The Texan had behind him the horse-riding
> tradition of the more literal than figurative "cava-
> lier South." In the lower part of Texas he met the
> herd-owning Spanish *caballero*—which word also
> means "horseman." He met the Spaniard's *va-
> quero,* the mounted worker with cows. He met
> the ranching industry of the open range, appropri-

[10] Durham and Jones, *The Negro Cowboys,* p. 1. (© 1965 by Philip
Durham and Everett L. Jones. By permission of Dodd, Mead &
Company, Inc.)

121

ated it, and shortly thereafter began extending it beyond the limits of the wildest initial dream. The coming together, not in blood but in place and occupation, of this Anglo-American, this Spanish owner, and this Mexican vaquero produced the Texas cowboy—a blend, a type, new to the world. The cow that called forth both him and the industry he represented was the mother of the Texas Longhorn.[11]

The Spanish word for cow is *vaca,* and a man who works with cows is a vaquero. Vaquero, as used in the Southwest, referred to any cowboy, but particularly Mexican cowboys. In the Northwest, vaquero became buckaroo; similarly, many Spanish terms were employed, though in slightly altered form, by men who adopted the techniques and equipment of people of a Spanish-American cultural heritage. In his book, *The Horsemen of the Americas and the Literature They Inspired* (p. 96), Edward Larocque Tinker examines the cowboy's vocabulary which:

> . . . is still generously peppered, in the Southwest, with Spanish words. He wears a *sombrero* and *chaps* (chaparreros), his stirrups are protected by *tapacieros,* and his lariat (from la riata) has a *hondo* on the end, he rides a bronco when he works a *rodeo,* and disciplines it with a *quirt.* His saddle has *cinchas, latigos,* and *alforjas,* he calls his string of ponies a *remuda* and the equine stock of a ranch a *caballada,* which he often shortens to cavvy. He has twisted the word *mesteno* into mustang, the generic term for the descendants of Spanish horses, and savvy, a corruption of *sabe,* is understood by everyone . . . .

The nomadic Plains Indians were, essentially, cattlemen. Their native cattle, essential to their existence, was the buf-

[11] Dobie, *The Longhorns,* p. xiv. (© 1941 J. Frank Dobie. By permission of Little, Brown and Co.)

falo. The transition to cowboy was relatively easy for the Indian, much easier than that to farmer or to city-dweller. Herding and grazing of cattle is a major industry on western reservation lands, and the American Indian is an important source of experienced and knowledgeable ranch hands in the West today.

Abilene, Kansas was the first of the cow towns. The Kansas Pacific was the first railroad to link these cow towns with northern markets; and the first shipment of Texas cattle arrived in Chicago from Abilene on September 5, 1867. For the next two decades, Texas longhorns were driven north to the railroad towns in Kansas and Nebraska, the mining camps of Colorado and the Indian reservations of Montana. The longhorn was also used to stock the northern ranges of Wyoming and Montana.

The cattle industry, which spread throughout the grass-lands of the West following the Civil War, originated in southern Texas in the region of the Nueces River Valley. Semi-wild longhorns, descendants of early Spanish cattle, thrived and multiplied in this region which provided almost ideal conditions. The climate was mild; grass remained green throughout most of the year; sufficient water was available; and occasional clumps of timber offered shade and protection. Few natural enemies existed, since the nomadic Plains Indians did not hunt that far south.

Veterans, mostly Confederate, returning from the Civil War, were attracted to this region beyond the settled towns and farms of east Texas. A man could become a rancher with little capital. The grass was free and so were the cattle. To establish ownership, he had to brand them, but this required a horse—the mustang, the proud and spirited animal from which came the cow pony. Frank Dobie describes the best of them as "tameless, and swift. . . . Their essence was the spirit of freedom."

Harry S. Drago, in his book, *Great American Cattle Trails,* maintains that the longhorn and the mustang must be regarded as inseparable.

The Longhorns have often been placed in the category of semi-domesticated animals, an opinion seldom shared by men who depended on them for their livelihood and who, presumably, were best acquainted with them. The mustang gave man an ascendancy of a sort over the Longhorns; he could herd and drive them but he could not break their will . . . . The Longhorn was dominated by its ingrained compulsion for freedom, and it could not be bred out . . . . He could scratch a living where other cattle would have starved; his hoofs were hard and distance meant nothing to him when he was going to water—often thirty-five miles or more. In his semiwild state, he was a savage fighter, fearing nothing that walked on four legs. When man pitted the mustang against the Longhorn, it was a case of steel meeting steel, for in spirit they were two of a kind.[12]

Though his brand might be on thousands of head of longhorn cattle, a Texas rancher would realize no profit from them unless he found a market. A few attempts were made in 1866, immediately following the Civil War, to drive the cattle to railroads in Missouri; but these drives were generally unsuccessful. Farmers opposed the drovers, fearing the introduction of Texas fever or "blackleg" among their own cattle. Cattle thieves took their toll, and the timbered country reduced the herds considerably.

It was at this time, however, that railroads were crossing the Missouri River and pushing out onto the Great Plains offering a direct route across sparsely settled grasslands. Cattle which brought only $3 to $5 per head in Texas would sell for as much as $40 or $50 in the North where beef was scarce and cities were growing rapidly as a result of increased European immigration and the effects of the Industrial Revolution.

[12] Pp. 80–1. (By permission of Dodd, Mead & Co., Inc. © 1965 by Harry Sinclair Drago.)

The ingenuity of Joseph G. McCoy, an Illinois cattleman, effected a union between northern markets, Texas cattle, and rail transportation to bring about the era of the long drive. McCoy conceived of the idea of establishing some accessible point where railroads and cattle trails could meet unmolested by angry farmers or cattle thieves and unhindered by geography. The location chosen for the meeting point between Texas drovers and Eastern buyers was on the newly constructed Kansas Pacific Railroad. Far enough west to be away from settled areas and to provide sufficient grassland to hold many cattle, and yet far enough east to provide a good depot for the cattle business. Abilene, Kansas was selected by McCoy to become the first "cow town."

Abilene grew from a dozen dirt-roofed log huts, whose only saloon keeper sold prairie dogs to Eastern tourists to provide himself an income, to a prosperous prairie city of four hotels, ten boarding houses, five drygoods and clothing stores, ten saloons, and numerous other businesses by 1870. Floyd Benjamin Streeter, in his book, *Prairie Trails and Cow Towns,* explains how Abilene was named.

> The town of Abilene was laid out in 1860 on land belonging to C. H. Thompson who had moved into the county from Leavenworth in the spring of that year. The name of the future cattle market was Biblical in origin, though this never would have been suspected after the cattle trade reached its height. When a name for the town was under consideration, Thompson asked Tim Hersey, his neighbor on the other side of Mud Creek, to suggest a name.
>
> "No," was the reply, "let my wife do it; she is a great reader."
>
> Mrs. Hersey knew her Bible from cover to cover. When the question of a name was referred to her, she turned to the third chapter of Luke, first Verse, and read, "Now in the fifteenth year of the reign of Tiberius Caesar, Pontius Pilate being gov-

> ernor of Judea . . . . and Lysanias, tetrarch of
> Abilene." Looking up, she said, "Call the town
> 'Abilene.' It means 'City of the Plains,' and that
> exactly describes the location." [13]

Abilene, marking the terminus of the Chisolm Trail, was supplanted by other cow towns farther west—Dodge City and Ogallala on the Western Trail and Cheyenne on the Goodnight-Loving Trail. The farther west a cow town was located, the tougher became its reputation, as illustrated by the following anecdote from *Prairie Trails and Cow Towns*:

> A drunken cowboy got aboard a Santa Fe train
> at Newton. When the conductor asked him for the
> fare, the cowpuncher handed him a handful of
> money.
> "Where do you want to go?" asked the conductor.
> "To Hell," replied the cowboy.
> "Well, give me $2.50 and get off at Dodge." [14]

The earlier cattle drives were conducted by professional drovers who purchased Texas cattle on credit and drove them north to the railroads. Later, ranchers either drove their own herds, or more often hired a competent trail boss. The long drive would begin early in the spring when grass and water were available along the trail, and as soon as the herds could be rounded up from the open ranges. As the drovers gained experience, the trail herds became larger; and it was found that about the same number of men could as easily handle a herd of 2,500 as it could a smaller one of 1,000. As trail drives became more routine, it was not unusual for herds to follow within a day of each other on the same trail or to be within sight of one another at many times, particularly at river crossings. And, as trail drives became longer, driving

[13] Streeter, Floyd Benjamin, *Prairie Trails and Cow Towns*, Devin-Adair & Co., 1963, p. 70.
[14] *Ibid.*, p. 155.

into the northern rangelands, it became necessary to identify the cattle with a special trail brand.

A trail-driving crew consisted of a foreman or a professional drover who directed the drive, approximately eight trail hands chosen for dependability and loyalty as much as for their ability, one or two horse herders ar wranglers who were placed in charge of the *remuda* or "cavvie yard" as the remuda de caballos was called, and a cook. Everett Dick's chapter, "The Long Drive," in *Vanguards of the Frontier*, describes a good cook as a gold mine to a drover.

> . . . for he would do more toward keeping up the morale of a trail crew than anyone else. He had to be not only a good cook but an expert bullwhacker or mule-skinner as well, for some wagons were pulled by oxen while horses furnished the motive power for others. The cook often was a hard character with a record of his own. He might be either Spanish or Negro with a notch or two on his gun. He was called the "old woman" by the crew, but he certainly was no lady if he were to be judged by his language.[15]

A man's ranking was indicated by the position he was assigned with the herd as it strung out along the trail. The position of most responsibility was "point." Two men, one on each side of the herd "pointed herd" as they rode abreast of the leaders; theirs was a position of importance especially in controlling a stampede. About a third of the way back on each side of the herd were the swing riders. These two men would be about fifty feet from each other which was the width of the herd at that point. Two flank riders followed another third of the way back and the most undesirable position was that of "riding drag" or bringing up the rear of the herd. The three men of least experience, other than the

[15] From *Vanguards of the Frontier* (p. 457) by Everett Dick. (By permission of University of Nebraska Press, © 1941.)

wranglers, were assigned "drag" and it was in this position that a man ate the dust of the entire herd while attempting to drive the slower, lazier, more stubborn or lame cattle.

The job least respected among the more experienced trail hands was that of wrangler, usually assigned to the youngest member of the crew. Every cowboy was allotted at least five horses, and these together comprised the remuda assigned to the wrangler's care. His was also the task of hobbling all the horses at night which were not being used in the night guard or kept close by the trail hands for immediate use in such an emergency as a stampede. The best compliment given a wrangler was to say "he never lost a horse."

One of the first things a newly assembled trail crew did was to pick their mounts from the remuda. The foreman selected all his mounts first, perhaps as many as a dozen, and his knowedge of horses was evident in the ones he selected. Each hand was then allowed to pick one horse at a time by turns until only the least desirable ponies were left, usually pintos. An experienced cowboy know this freak of color in range-bred horses was the result of in-breeding which led to a physical and mental deterioration in the horse.

The chuck wagon completed the outfit. It was canvas covered and usually a well-built four-wheeled wagon, though some crews used two-wheeled carts for chuck wagons. A water barrel was fastened inside the wagon bed and a spigot run outside so that water could be easily obtained. A barrel of water would last the crew at least two days on the trail. A chuck box, mounted on back of the wagon, was divided into compartments to hold all the cook's utensils. His work table was a leaf lowered from the chuck box. Wood and dry cow chips were thrown into the "caboose," a cowhide tied by the four corners and hanging loose under the wagon. A box was built onto the front of the wagon to carry tools, pieces of rawhide, and all sorts of odds and ends which would come in handy during the drive.

The chuck wagon was the outfit's headquarters, and it carried all the papers of the foreman, the hands' sleeping equipment and few personal possessions, and a thirty-day supply of provisions. Supply points and the few towns on the trail provided the cook opportunities to replenish the provisions when necessary. The cook was the first man up in the morning, and after breakfast he drove the chuck wagon on ahead of the herd to a site designated by the foreman to prepare the noon meal. The same process was repeated for the evening meal.

Twenty miles per day was about the average distance covered on a drive. But in the first several days on the trail, thirty to thirty-five miles were handled the first nights; lost weight would be quickly regained in succeeding days of grazing along the trail. It was also desirable, when beginning the drive, to move the cattle and remuda away from familiar range as soon as possible; and the longer hours on the trail helped to break the cattle to the drive.

There was actually no "driving" involved in a long drive. The herd trailed out behind the leaders—who usually led the entire distance—and moved of their own free will at about two or three miles per hour. The instructions given by the foreman of Andy Adams' crew on April 1, 1882, the day this particular drive began, provide an excellent example of what was expected of each man.

> "Boys, the secret of trailing cattle is never to let your herd know that they are under restraint. Let everything that is done be done voluntarily by the cattle. From the moment you let them off the bed ground in the morning until they are bedded at night, never let a cow take a step, except in the direction of its destination. In this manner you can loaf away the day, and cover from fifteen to twenty miles, and the herd in the mean time will enjoy all the freedom of an open range. Of course, it's long, tiresome hours to the men; but the condition of the herd and saddle stock demands sacrifices on our part, if any have to be made. And I want to caution you younger boys about your

> horses; there is such a thing as having ten horses in your string, and at the same time being afoot. You are well mounted, and on the condition of the remuda depends the success and safety of the herd. Accidents will happen to horses, but don't let it be your fault; keep your saddle blankets dry and clean, for no better word can be spoken of a man than that he is careful of his horses. Ordinarily a man might get along with six or eight horses, but in such emergencies as we are liable to meet, we have not a horse to spare, and a man afoot is useless." [16]

Though the foreman might not stand night guard duty as much as his men, he made up for it by riding almost double the distance of his hands by constant circling of the herd as it grazed forward. The foreman would not leave the herd until it was bedded down at night, and he was often the man who awakened the cook the next morning. It was the foreman who led the herd from the bed ground just before dawn.

At dusk, the cattle were grazed around in a large circle in preparation for bringing them to the bed ground. The foreman tried to select an area of old dry grass for the bed ground and one which was elevated enough to catch any breezes. Cattle were bedded down only after being well watered and well grazed. Hunger and thirst were probably the reasons responsible for stampedes.

The greatest problem was that of stampedes, which were the natural result of fear. A dark or humid night, a rainstorm and lightning, hungry and thirsty cattle, a sudden noise, any of these might cause a stampede. It was always several days before the cattle would settle down again and the men could relax their vigil somewhat. Frank Collinson, who began his career with cattle at the age of seventeen, described a stampede in his book, *Life in the Saddle.*

[16] From *The Log of a Cowboy* (pp. 28–9) by Andy Adams. (By permission of University of Nebraska Press, © 1965.)

. . . Sometimes on a clear night the cattle would be bedded down, when the air would suddenly become warm and still. Then distant thunder could be heard and phosphorous would shine on the long horns of the cattle and on the horses' ears. Then we knew a storm was brewing. Suddenly like a streak of lightning every steer jumped to its feet and was away on the run. The entire herd seemed to move like one huge animal.

In such instances the cowboys tried to keep in the lead so that the steers could eventually be turned in a circle. If the lightning and thunder and rain continued, the frightened animals would keep running for several miles.

Finally when they were herded there was water standing everywhere, and it was difficult or impossible to bed them again. Then the cowboys, cold and miserable, and often wet to the skin, stood guard the remainder of the night. Maybe one or two broke into song, but it took a brave lad to sing under such conditions.

The big job awaited us at the crack of dawn. We first counted the cattle, and if any were gone, we followed their tracks on fresh horses. Maybe they were not far off—maybe they were twenty miles; but get them we had to do, even if they were half way back to the home range.[17]

A stampede might take its toll of men as well as of cattle and then it was the cook's sorrowful duty to breakout the shovel from the chuck wagon. But more often a stampede was just another incident to "story about" or on which to philosophize.

Equally to be feared was a "dry drive." This would occur while driving the herd through a particularly arid stretch of

[17] From *Life in the Saddle* (pp. 36–6) by Frank Collinson, edited and arranged by Mary Whatley Clarke. (© 1963 by the University of Oklahoma Press.)

the trail where water was available only at widely separated intervals. Or, a dry drive might be the result of a summer drought in a region normally offering abundant watering points. The result of a dry drive is described by Andy Adams.

> . . . We had not been on the trail over two hours before the heat became almost unbearable to man and beast. Had it not been for the condition of the herd, all might yet have gone well; but over three days had now elapsed without water for the cattle, and they became feverish and ungovernable. The lead cattle turned back several times, wandering aimlessly in any direction, and it was with considerable difficulty that the herd could be held on the trail. The rear overtook the lead, and the cattle gradually lost all semblance of a trail herd . . . [they] congregated into a mass of unmanageable animals, milling and lowing in their fever and thirst . . . . No sooner was the milling stopped than they would surge hither and yon, sometimes half a mile, as ungovernable as the waves of an ocean. After wasting several hours in this manner, they finally turned back over the trail, and the utmost efforts of every man in the outfit failed to check them. We threw our ropes in their faces, and when this failed, we resorted to shooting; but in defiance of the fusillade and the smoke they walked sullenly through the line of horsemen across their front. Six-shooters were discharged so close to the leaders' face as to singe their hair, yet, under a noonday sun, they disregarded this and every other device to turn them, and passed wholly out of our control. In a number of instances wild steers deliberately walked against our horses, and then for the first time a fact dawned on us that chilled the marrow in our bones,—*the herd was going blind*.[18]

[18] From *The Log of a Cowboy* (pp. 62–4) by Andy Adams. (By permission of University of Nebraska Press, © 1965.)

The usual daily routine was monotonous. After long hours in the saddle under a hot sun, breathing dust, with no one to talk to except himself or the cattle, the drover welcomed the appearance of an occasional stranger. He might be the foreman of a nearby trail herd come to discuss conditions along the trail—and to sample the cook's talents. The stranger might be an Indian come to exact toll in the form of cattle for the right to cross reservation lands, or he might be a "trail cutter" come to cut range cattle from the herd.

As a trail herd made its way north, cattle other than those originally gathered for the drive, would be absorbed into the herd. If these strays were not cut out by trail cutters, the honest foreman would keep an account of their brands when he delivered the herd and would reimburse the rightful owners. But in a few instances, cattle thieves would operate in the guise of trail cutters. It was on such occasions that a good foreman drew upon his knowledge of brands to detect false credentials.

One of the major geographic obstacles encountered along the trails were the rivers: the Colorado, Brazos, Red, Canadian, Cimarron, Arkansas, and more if the herd were being driven into northern ranges or to northern railroads. The crossing of one of these rivers was always a well-planned undertaking for, even at best, crossing several thousand head of cattle would be time consuming. At worst, a crossing could involve cattle bogged in quicksand or carried away by strong currents. An experienced foreman sought a crossing which offered a firm bottom to the river, preferably a rocky one (as shallow a crossing as possible) and one offering gradual slopes on each bank. The cowboys preferred to keep the cattle from drinking water until they approached the river to be crossed. Hours and even days could be wasted just trying to get a few cattle to take the lead in crossing so that the remainder of the herd would follow. Once in the river, the cowboys had to keep the herd moving in order to prevent milling or turning back in mid-stream or the scattering of cattle as they left the water at dozens of points up and down the river.

Every man in the trail crew was eager to cross the Arkansas or the Platte Rivers, if the cow town on the other side was the objective of their long drive. Reaching Abilene, Dodge City, Ogallala, Cheyenne meant that after several months, the foreman or drover could at last turn the cattle over to the ranch owner, whose last words before the drive began had been, "I'll see you in. . . ." To the cook, the end of the trail provided an opportunity to taste somebody else's grub for a change. The young horse wranglers looked forward to their first night in a cow town and were not usually disappointed. The experienced trail hands anticipated visiting a barber shop with a bathtub, a gambling hall, and a saloon—though, not necessarily in that order.

> On reaching Dodge, we rode up to the Wright House, where [the foreman] met us and directed our cavalcade across the railroad to a livery stable . . . . We unsaddled and turned our horses into a large corral, and while we were in the office of the livery, surrendering our artillery, [the foreman] came in and handed each of us twenty-five dollars in gold, warning us that when that was gone no more would be advanced. On receipt of the money, we scattered like partridges before a gunner. Within an hour or two, we began to return to the stable by ones and twos, and were stowing into our saddle pockets our purchases, which ran from needles and thread to .45 cartridges, every mother's son reflecting the art of the barber, [one of the cowboys] had his blond mustaches blackened, waxed, and curled like a French dancing master. . . .
>
> After packing away our plunder, we sauntered around town, drinking moderately, and visiting the various saloons and gambling houses . . . .[19]

[19] From *The Log of a Cowboy* (pp. 198–9) by Andy Adams. (By permission of University of Nebraska Press, © 1965.)

After the cattle and the remuda were sold and the men had spent two-thirds of their pay on new clothes, boots, and hats, it came time to head back to Texas and routine ranch duties while awaiting the next long drive north. The pleasant remembrances of the novelties of a trail drive tended to displace the memory of the monotony and boredom of which most of the drive consisted. Driving cattle by moonlight might be such an occurrence to inspire enjoyable recollections. With the cook's lantern carried as a beacon by a point rider, a herd of cattle well broken to the trail strung out for a mile behind; and a drag rider bringing up the rear with the singing of:

> Ip-e-la-ago, go 'long little doggie,
> You'll make a beef-steer by-and-by.[20]

A cowboy would remember, as did Andy Adams:

> . . . in the stillness of those splendid July nights we could hear the point men chatting across the lead in front, while in the rear, the rattling of our heavily loaded wagon and, the whistling of the horse wrangler to his charges reached our ears. The swing men were scattered so far apart there was no chance for conversation amongst us, but every once in a while a song would be started, and as it surged up and down the line, every voice, good, bad, and indifferent, joined in.[21]

End of the Open Range

The first northern ranches were products of the emigrant trade. These road ranches supplied the Oregon or California-bound emigrant with fresh stock. One fat and well-conditioned work steer might be exchanged for two trail-worn ones.

[20] [21] From *The Log of a Cowboy* (pp. 313–14) by Andy Adams. (By permission of University of Nebraska Press, © 1965.)

A milk cow brought from a midwestern farm would be traded for needed provisions by her owner who despaired of ever reaching Oregon with the cow still alive, but who was in need of flour. Thus were begun in the 1840's and 1850's the ranches of the northern Great Plains and valleys of the Rocky Mountains. These ranches were further stocked, in the 1870's and 1880's with longhorns driven up from Texas. These early ranchers of Wyoming, Colorado, and Montana were usually old mountain men who, after the decline of the fur trade, were reluctant to leave the country in which they had trapped and traded for twenty years.

John Iliff, the first of the cattle kings of the northern ranges, got his start from the stock of gold-seekers heading toward the mines of Colorado beginning in 1858–59. He built his herd from purchases of longhorns brought up the Goodnight-Loving and Western cattle trails from Texas. By 1861, Iliff was supplying the mining towns with beef from a herd grazing his range which extended for over seventy-five miles up and down the South Platte River.

Longhorns driven up the Bozeman Trail provided the base for herds in southwestern Montana and a source of beef for the mining towns near Bozeman and Helena. Many Texas cowboys remained in these northern ranching regions, lured by unoccupied rangelands and the demand for experienced cowhands.

The range and ranch cattle industry spread throughout the Great Plains and by the 1880's occupied nearly all the grasslands of that vast area so naturally suited to raising cattle. Walter Prescott Webb recognized four steps in the development of this industry, "perhaps the most unique and distinctive institution that America has produced."

> The first step was made when the Spaniards and Mexicans established their ranches in the Nueces country of southern Texas, where natural conditions produced a hardy breed of cattle that could grow wild; the second step occurred when the

Texans took over these herds and learned to handle them in the only way they could have been handled—on horseback; the third step was taken when the cattle were driven northward to market; the fourth came when a permanent depot was set up at Abilene which enabled trail-driving to become standardized; the fifth took place when the overflow from the trail went west to the free grass of the Great Plains.[22]

The process of establishing a ranch on the northern ranges was described to the National Stock Growers' Convention in Chicago in 1886 by a successful Wyoming rancher.

Except for the money to purchase the cattle, investment was slight enough. A homestead entry of 160 acres along some stream was selected as the basis for operations. If there was wild hay on the land, forage for the riding stock was assured. Ranch houses and corrals might come later, but many an early cattleman spent the first season or two in a dugout cut in the hillside near the creek with a similar one close by for sheltering his horses in the worst storms. Beef from his herd, bacon, beans, and coffee brought by pack horse from the nearest settlement, constituted the bill of fare.[23]

The ranching industry entered its boom period after the Civil War; and from approximately 1870 until 1885, the Great Plains was a region of open range, an empire of grass. The Buffalo, New York, *Live Stock Journal* proclaimed, in 1875, that "Cotton was once crowned king but grass is now. . . . If grass is King, the Rocky Mountain region is its throne and fortunate indeed are those who possess it." But, for the most part, the rancher did not possess it.

[22] Webb, *op. cit.,* p. 224.
[23] Osgood, *Day of the Cattlemen,* p. 49. (© 1929 by the University of Minnesota, renewed by Ernest Staples Osgood. All rights reserved.)

The range, the term applied to open and unfenced grass-lands, was used by the rancher and each possessed what was recognized by his neighbors as "range rights." Contrary to the understanding of many an Eastern tenderfoot or foreign investor in western cattle, range rights did not constitute legal ownership of portions of rangelands. When the farmer's frontier pushed out onto the grasslands; and he took up a homestead of 160 acres—or in the more arid regions at a later date, 320 acres—his was recognized as legal possession of the land. Many ranchers, utilizing tactics of the enemy, homesteaded 160 acres along the stream where the ranch headquarters were located and had their cowboys take up more homesteads which the rancher then purchased.

The rancher's range rights had meant his right to a portion of a stream and all the rangeland back from that stream to the divide which marked the boundary between one stream valley and the next. Claims upon a distance of frontage along a stream therefore entitled a rancher to the rangeland back of the stream, and he had access to the two basic require-ments—grass and water. No attempt was made by the ranchers to fence off portions of rangelands. Range cattle grazed freely, intermingling with stock of other herds. Cow-boys might occasionally, as a neighborly act, throw cattle back across the divide onto their home range, but the calf roundup in the spring would separate the cattle for the purpose of branding and marking calves. The full roundup would catch any strays missed in the spring.

A single rancher did not conduct his own roundup, but participated with his neighbors in a roundup of an entire district involving the ranges of a number of ranchers. Roundups required cooperative efforts and organization. The cattlemen of a district would meet to select one of their number as a general superintendent of the roundup; this was an experienced rancher in whose judgment the other ranchers had confidence. The superintendent's authority and instruc-tions were respected by the ranchers and cowboys. Every rancher whose range was included in the roundup contributed something according to the size of his outfit, chuck wagons, food, horse remudas, gear and equipment.

Each range in the district to be covered by the roundup was worked in succession. Cowboys fanned out over a range and worked all the cattle toward the center, where the size of the herd grew larger as did the number of brands represented. The man whose range was being worked was given the first "cut." All the cows which bore his brand were cut out of the asssembled herd, and the calves that followed were branded and marked. As the roundup proceeded onto the next range, he would hold his cattle in a separate herd. Until the introduction of barbed wire in the mid-1870's, making possible the erection of corrals, cowboys had to guard the herds day and night.

Though his occupation might succeed best in isolation from neighbors and an absence of enforced governmental regulations, the cattleman was eventually forced to seek the cooperation of his fellow ranchers. In every western state has been created some type of cattlemen's organization. In his book, *The Day of the Cattleman,* Ernest Staples Osgood lists three common aims of the cattle community.

> . . . first, to preserve the individual's ownership in his herd and its increase; second, to afford protection to the individual's herd; and third, to control the grazing of the public domain in order to prevent overcrowding.[24]

As a member of a group, the cattleman could protect his property, which was cattle. A uniform system of branding, requiring the registration of brands, helped to protect the rancher from thieves. A cattlemen's protective association could hire brand inspectors to check the legitimacy of brands as stock was brought to markets and shipping points. The association hired detectives to apprehend cattle thieves.

[24] P. 115. (© 1929 by the University of Minnesota, renewed by Ernest Staples Osgood. All rights reserved.)

Herds brought up from Texas were inspected for disease, particularly Texas Fever, and these herds were in some instances prevented from entering northern ranges. The cattlemen's organizations could secure favorable railroad rates for shipping cattle to eastern markets, bargain with Indian agents for grazing privileges on reservation lands, or influence lawmaking bodies to pass legislation favorable to the cattle industry. Working cooperatively, the cattlemen protected valuable rangelands from grass fires and punished those guilty of setting them.

His study of the rise and development of cattlemen's organization has prompted Professor Osgood to observe:

> . . . one can watch the characteristic frontier individualism succumb to the equally characteristic frontier need for group effort, the evolution of custom into law, and the appearance of certain institutions, which became part of the economic and social structure of the Far West.[25]

The most difficult problem facing the cattleman was that of controlling the grazing on lands which did not belong to him, but on which he relied for grazing his own stock. Such lands were part of the public domain. This problem, along with such factors as the introduction of barbed wire, homesteading on the public domain, and the severe weather conditions of the mid-1880's led to the passing of the rancher's frontier.

Speculation by Eastern investors helped to overstock the ranges. Such articles as the following published in the *Breeder's Gazette* in 1883, were partly responsible for the over-grazing of western rangelands:

How Cattlemen Grow Rich

A good sized steer, when it is fit for the butcher market will bring from $45 to $60. The same

[25] *Ibid.,* p. 117.

animal at its birth was worth but $5.00. He was run on the plains and cropped the grass from the public domain for four or five years, and now, with scarcely any expense to his owner, is worth forty dollars more than when he started on his pilgrimage. A thousand of these animals are kept nearly as cheaply as a single one, so with a thousand as a starter and with an investment of but $5,000 in the start, in four years the stock raiser has made from $40,000 to $45,000, allow $5,000 for his current expenses which he has been going on and he still has $35,000 and even $45,000 for a net profit. That is all there is of the problem and that is why our cattlemen grow rich.[26]

When disaster came, it was the big Eastern investor and the foreign speculator who suffered the greatest financial losses, and the resulting withdrawal of capital from the cattle industry brought the boom to an end.

Wintering cattle on the open range was a gamble, and to many Eastern critics, was inhumane as well. If the previous summer feeding had been poor due to drought or overstocked ranges, the cattle would lack the vitality necessary to survive even an average winter on the open range. And the northern ranges were flooded with cattle in the summer of 1885. In addition to the burden of native stock, the grasslands had to support hundreds of thousands of Eastern cattle unused to rustling forage on their own along some windswept ridge. That summer, President Cleveland had ordered the removal of 200,000 head from the Cheyenne-Arapahoe reservation lands in Indian Territory. Their owners, who had experienced a severely dry summer, sent the cattle to northern ranges to winter. Even a normal winter resulted in losses of five to ten per cent of the herds, but the winter of 1885–86 was one of the severest in the history of the Great Plains.

The next spring cattlemen reckoned their losses at 85 per cent of their herds! And to such a loss was added the prospect

[26] *Ibid.*, pp. 85–6.

of declining cattle prices. In their attempt to get out of the cattle business, Southwestern cattlemen had flooded the market with their herds. Cattle were bringing the lowest prices in the history of the open range. A few Montana and Wyoming cattlemen drove small herds of young stock to the agricultural areas of those territories where small ranchers had feed to spare, or they shipped them to farmers in eastern Nebraska and Iowa. Such actions foretold the changes which were to take place in the cattle industry.

The summer of 1886 was hot and dry, grass was thin, and the remaining cattle were in poor condition to face the coming winter. Professor Osgood, utilizing newspaper accounts of the time, described that winter:

> In the latter part of November, there was a heavy fall of snow, so heavy that in many places the cattle could not get down to the grass. Gloomy reports began to come in from all sections. Those who had put up hay fed all they could, the rest whose cattle were all out on the ranges prayed for a chinook. It came, early in January, booming up from the southwest, melting the snow and blowing the exposed ridges bare. Men took heart, they might get through without disaster. But the odds were against them for from the twenty-eighth of January to the thirtieth, the Northwest was swept by a blizzard such as the ranges had never before experienced. Down from the north, came a terrific wind before which the cattle drifted aimlessly or sought shelter in the coulees. A merciless cold locked up every bit of the poor grazing that remained. Men were forced to keep to the ranch houses for weeks as the bitter cold and the high winds scourged the range. They dared not think of the tragedy that was being enacted outside. Unacclimated "dogies" and young stock from Iowa and Wisconsin huddled in the quaking aspens and cottonwoods to die. Dry cows and steers, whose resistance was greater, lingered on. One

morning the inhabitants on the outskirts of Great
Falls looked out through the swirl of snow to see
the gaunt, reeling figures of the leaders of a herd
of five thousand that had drifted down to the
frozen Missouri from the north. Inhabitants of
ranch houses tried not to hear the noises that
came from beyond the corrals. The longing for
another chinook that never arrived became the
yearning for a miracle. Old-timers, who were
hardened to range losses, were in a state of abso-
lute panic. . . . The disaster was complete.[27]

The frontier of the open range was gone. Those portions
not occupied by farmers with their windmills and barbed
wire remained open for another decade or two as remnants
of a passing frontier; but cattlemen realized that they could
not rely upon the open range—their stock had to be fed
through the winter. Herds that had survived the disasters of
1885 and 1886 were drastically reduced. As the ranges recovered, cattlemen fenced them into summer and winter
pastures and installed windmills to pump water to those
sections on which they grew hay to be cut and stored for
winter feeding. In the decade 1880–1890 the acreage set
aside for the cultivation of hay increased more than tenfold
marking the decline of the range cattle industry and the
passing of the cowboy as a frontier figure.

The Industrial Revolution and the approaching settlers'
frontier signalled the end of the open range. Old-time cowboys looked back on a way of life at a time when a cowboy
had been, essentially, a man who worked with cows.

Cowboys don't have as soft a time as they did.
I remember when we sat around the fire the winter through and didn't do a lick of work for five
or six months of the year, except to chop a little
wood to build a fire to keep warm by. Now we
go on the general roundup, then the calf roundup,

[27] *Ibid.,* pp. 220–1.

then comes haying—something that the old-time cowboy never dreamed of—then the beef roundup and the fall calf roundup and gathering bulls and weak cows, and after all this, a winter of feeding hay. I tell you times have changed. You didn't hear the sound of a mowing machine in this country ten years ago. We didn't have any hay and the man who thinks he is going to strike a soft job now in a cow camp is woefully left.[28]

Bibliography

Adams, Andy	*The Log of a Cowboy* University of Nebraska Press, Lincoln, Neb.	1965 ed.
Adams, Ramon	*Western Words* University of Oklahoma Press, Norman, Okla.	1944 ed.
Bronson, Edgar Beecher	*Reminiscences of a Ranchman* University of Nebraska Press, Lincoln, Neb.	1962
Collinson, Frank	*Life in the Saddle* University of Oklahoma Press, Norman, Okla.	1963 ed.
Dale, Edward Everett	*The Range Cattle Industry* University of Oklahoma Press, Norman, Okla.	1960 ed.
Dick, Everett	*Vanguards of the Frontier* University of Nebraska Press, Lincoln, Neb.	1941 ed.
Dobie, J. Frank	*Cow People* Little, Brown, Boston, Mass.	1964 ed.
Dobie, J. Frank	*The Longhorns* Grosset & Dunlap, New York, N.Y.	1941 ed.
Drago, Harry Sinclair	*Great American Cattle Trails* Dodd, Mead, New York, N.Y.	1965 ed.
Durham, Philip and Jones, Everett L.	*The Negro Cowboys* Dodd, Mead, New York, N.Y.	1965 ed.
Frantz, Joe B. and Choate, Ernest J.	*The American Cowboy* University of Oklahoma Press, Norman, Okla.	1955 ed.

[28] *Ibid.*, p. 229.

Osgood,
  Ernest Staples
	The Day of the Cattleman
	University of Chicago Press,
	  Chicago, Ill.
		1957 ed.

Russell, Charles M.	*Trails Plowed Under* Doubleday, Garden City, N.Y.	1927 ed.
Sandoz, Mari	*The Cattlemen* Hastings House, New York, N.Y.	1958 ed.
Streeter, Benjamin Floyd	*Prairie Trails & Cow Towns* Devin-Adair, New York, N.Y.	1963 ed.

Tinker,
  Edward Larocque
	The Horsemen of the Americas
	  and the Literature They Inspired
	Hastings House, New York, N.Y.
		1953 ed.

Webb, Walter Prescott	*The Great Plains* Grosset & Dunlap, New York, N.Y.	1931 ed.

Periodicals

Adams, Ramon	"A Cowman's Philosophy" *The American West*, Vol. II, No. 4	Fall, 1965
Lambert, Neal	"A Cowboy Writes to Owen Wister" *The American West*, Vol. II, No. 4	Fall, 1965
Rojas, Arnold R.	"The Vaquero" *The American West*, Vol. I, No. 2	Spring, 1964
Ulph, Owen C.	"Cowhands, Cow Horses, and Cows" *The American West*, Vol. III, No. 1	Winter, 1966

6 | The Pioneer Settlers

In his very authoritative and widely admired work, *The Old Northwest* (Vol. I, p. 1), R. C. Buley employs a quotation to introduce his story of Northwest settlement. The quotation is used here, however, to introduce the role of the major characters in a much larger saga—the pageant of the pioneer settler—a saga for which only the beginnings are found in the Old Northwest.

> A savage wilderness, resting in primaeval solitude, or inhabited only by a race whose practice it is when they migrate, to leave no trace behind, is suddenly opened to an eager multitude, who

pour in like the waters of the sea, and cover it with civilized life. The forest falls around them, and is consumed or converted into habitations; the ground is opened by the industrious plough-share—the comfortable house is raised, the rude wagon is built, and the spot where "yesterday" all was silent, save the beast and the bird, be-comes today the home of the woodsman—the center of human affections—the nucleus perhaps of an intelligent, social, virtuous community—the focus, where, it may be, light shall emanate to other parts of the world.

The Old Northwest

To the north of the Ohio River, stretching from Pennsyl-vania on the east to the Mississippi River on the west, and bounded on the north by Canada, lies a region known in American history as the Old Northwest. This territory was established as the first colony of the United States by the Ordinance of 1787. The attractiveness of the Northwest country and the troubled conditions in both the East and South combined to drive the frontier westward. Following the war with England in 1812, successive waves of a great migration poured into that region.

The environment of Old Northwest was one of variation and contrast. Running from the fringe of the plantation south to the edge of the Canadian frontier, it was a center of fusion for population elements from all corners of the thirteen states as well as Europe. Its colonial background was both British and French, and its borders contained some of the most for-midable aboriginal warriors in the world—the Winnebago, Sauk and Fox. The fertility of the soil ranged from rich prairie and flood plains to sand dunes and rock. In addition to containing rich mineral deposits, its vast resources of timber and water provided the birthplace of the American

147

fur trade. Here in the Old Northwest the uniquely American experiments in settlement and government took place—and established a pattern which emerged again and again as the great migration of pioneer settlers proceeded westward.

Much of the varied character of the Northwest resulted from the inherent diversity of its settlers. They came from all sections of the Atlantic seaboard and beyond the Fall Line. Some were traders, some were farmers and some defied classification.

Ray Allen Billington, among the greatest of all authorities on the West, suggests that the first flow of emigrants into the Old Northwest came largely from the South. Billington identified a number of conditions which promoted the Southern exodus including—the dislike of slavery; the rapid expansion of the plantation system which engulfed the western Carolinas, Georgia and eastern Tennessee during the postwar years and drove the small farmer from his land; and the distaste for aristocratic social distinctions which grew with the plantation system. The combination of these forces drove thousands of backcountry Southerners across the Ohio.

The Southern emigrants, by themselves, represented a wide economic diversity. The research of Dr. Buley revealed one family which arrived by boat from North Carolina with a young team of horses, a buggy, four farm wagons, a number of luxury household goods, including a piano, and a year's supply of groceries. Their intention was to bring as much comfort to the wilderness as possible. Not all were so fortunate. One contemporary writer recorded his observations of *another* couple from the same state.

> Behind the rest, some distance in the rear, comes the lonesome looking couple from *Old North Carolina*. They had evidently, from their appearance, ventured their all, such as it was, upon the enterprise. An old one-horse tumbril, with two high creaking wheels, and an old store box for a body—drawn by a lean pony of the preceding

generation, constituted their mode of conveyance. A bed, a spinning wheel, a pair of cards, a bag of dye stuff, and a few hanks of copperas colored cotton, with six sickly looking children, made up their stock in trade. As they moved slowly along, man walking before, and the wife behind, the tumbril, their lean pony occasionally stopping to crop the tall grass which stood by the way, it was evident to all who saw them, that they had long since arrived at that term of life which the magistrate alluded to, who married them, when he said "better for worse." [1]

Pioneer diversity was further compounded by other migratory sources. Traditionally, New England was a region of small, self-sufficient farmers. The introduction of the factory system of 1810, suggests Billington, started an economic revolution which forced the small farmer to abandon his self-sufficient economy and specialize in individual crops. The growth of New England textile mills, for example, created a demand for wool. Consequently, many landowners enlarged their farms and converted the fields into pasture land. The "sheep craze," as Billington defines it, swept through New England between the years 1825 to 1840, and those who lost their farms were left with the choice of going to work in one of the mills or moving west.

In addition to the problem of specialization, the Eastern farmer was faced with the importation of cheaply produced Western grains. By 1845, the cost of shipping one bushel of wheat from Chicago to New York via the Erie Canal was only twenty-five cents. Consequently, 1½ million bushels of wheat passed through Buffalo every year. The obvious result was an increased westward migration by the seaboard farmer.

The hardy New England emigrant was described by the same observer who noted the progress of the poverty-stricken couple from North Carolina. The New Englander provided an interesting contrast.

[1] Buley, *op. cit.*, p. 27.

> First in order, as he is always first when specula-
> tion is concerned, comes the hardy, enterprising
> New Englander. Of all the emigrants to the West,
> Brother Jonathan alone knows where he is going
> to—the cheapest mode of travel, and what he is
> going to do when he gets there; he alone has read
> the preemption laws, and knows what sum he
> must take with him, or notions in the way of
> trade, to secure a home in the wilderness. Already,
> before he gets there, he converses fluently about
> ranges, townships, and sections, has ascertained
> the number of acres in each sub-division, the
> amount reserved for schools, and is ready on his
> arrival to avail himself of his new position.[2]

Their conestogas (wagons) loaded down with household
belongings—the speculator and the dispossessed, the New
Englander and the Southerner, the businessman and the
farmer alike moved westward. Those from the Northeast
came over the Catskill and Genesee turnpikes or the National
and Wilderness roads, while those migrating from the South
passed through the Cumberland, the Saluda or Ward's gap.
The more fortunate came by water—from the north by way
of the Erie Canal and Great Lakes, while others traveled
inland by way of the Ohio, the Miami, Scioto, and Wabash
Rivers. In ever greater numbers, the pioneer settler continued to come from all quarters of the seaboard over crudely
developed routes into the northwestern wilderness. Billington
quoted one traveler on the National road in 1817 as saying:

> Old America seems to be breaking up and moving
> westward. We are seldom out of sight as we travel
> on this grand track, towards the Ohio, of family
> groups before and behind us.[3]

[2] *Ibid.,* p. 47.
[3] Billington, Ray, *Westward Expansion,* p. 295. (© 1963, by permission of Macmillan Co.)

All manner of humanity moved into the region and lived side by side, intermarrying and electing each other to office. Such conditions prompted R. C. Buley to note:

> In the hardships and necessary co-operations of frontier life the good qualities were brought out as well as the bad, and "narrow-nosed Yankee" and "shiftless Kaintuck" learned to recognize the useful traits of each other.[4]

Upon their arrival in the hostile wilderness, the settlers were confronted with problems which appeared insurmountable—the problems of food, shelter and survival. One pioneer wife, who had moved twice within the same year recorded her impressions of the trip to Indiana and the conditions which awaited her.

> On the 16th day of February, 1825, I, in company with Mr. Odell's family, left Wayne county, Indiana, to emigrate to the Wabash country. Our journey lasted fourteen days. We had rain every day, except two, during our trip. The men would cut brush on which to lay our beds, to sleep. Our clothes would be wet upon our backs in the mornin, sometimes. The country from White River to the Wabash was an unbroken wilderness, uninhabited, with the exception of a few Indians at Thorntown. We got along tolerably well, until we got this side Thorntown, when our wagon broke down . . . . The next morning . . . . I got on the horse, with my babe in my lap . . . . Sometimes it rained, and then it snowed, as fast as it could come down. I was on the horse from sunrise until dark, with a child in my arms, two years old. You may be sure that I was very much fatigued. The next day . . . my husband came with our goods. On the day following he was taken sick

[4] Buley, *op. cit.*, p. 48.

and kept down about six weeks. We thought he would die. We had no doctor, nor any medicine . . . . I was confined the 21st day of August, and could procure a nurse but for two days, when I had to get up and perform my work as best I could . . . . Another family came to the neighborhood, who had settled on Deer Creek . . . . who all got sick and lost a child . . . . They wanted me to wash for them, as they had no washing done for six weeks. I told them I would try; and I did try, and performed as large a day's work as ever I did, when my babe was but three weeks old. The next December my husband came up to Deer Creek, and built a cabin. February 15, 1826, we started for our new home . . . The weather was very cold, and the snow about a foot deep. We stopped at John Carey's, and got some fire—we had no matches those times. We drove up to the cabin; I crawled under the wall, scraped away the snow, and kindled a fire, while the men sawed out a door. The snow was about shoe-top deep in the house. We threw down some clapboards, and on them we placed our beds. We slept inside, and the hogs outside. The next morning the mud was as deep in our cabin as the snow had been the evening before. The weather was cold. We built a log-heap in our new cabin, but still we almost froze. My husband would hew puncheons all day, and chink our cabin at night. We were nearly three miles from our nearest neighbor. We brought corn-meal with us, sufficient, as we thought, to last until after planting; but it gave out, and I had to pound corn in an iron pot, with an iron wedge driven into the end of a hand-spike, and sift it through a basket-lid. We used the finest of the meal for breakfast, and the coarse for dinner and supper. We got our corn planted about the first of June, and then went to mill in a pirogue, down the Wabash, to a little corn-cracker . . . . I was taken sick about the first of July, and both our

children. I shook forty days with the ague . . . .
We then got some quinine, which stopped it for ten
days . . . . I never saw a woman, except one . . .
for three months.[5]

And yet, this woman was far more fortunate than most.
Her husband had preceded her some nine months before and
constructed a cabin so they could at least have shelter. When
most families arrived, their first chore was that of erecting
some sort of temporary shelter which normally took the form
of a three-sided dwelling, variously referred to as a lean-to,
pole-shed or half-faced camp. It consisted of two sturdy poles
placed in the ground about fourteen feet apart with the roof
slanting from the top of the poles all the way to the ground
on the north side. The south side was left open where a log
fire was kept burning night and day. The sides and roof were
covered with branches, brush, dried grass and clay mud,
while the interior of the shelter was lined with bearskins and
wolf pelts. In the two far corners of the shelter were beds
of dry leaves. The ones who arrived to find their cabin
already built were fortunate indeed.

In the year of 1816, one family migrated from Kentucky
to the Buckhorn Valley in southern Indiana near Little
Pigeon Creek. They arrived with nothing but the land on
which they stood; for even the team and wagon which trans-
ported them had been rented. The first labor of that family—
consisting of Tom Lincoln, his wife Nancy, his daughter
Sarah and his seven-year-old son Abraham—was to join in
the construction of an open-faced shelter, exactly like the
one described above, where they lived for one full year before
building a cabin.

When the settlers decided it was time for building their
10x20 foot log cabin, many of them had to do the work alone.
But most often it was a cooperative effort called a cabin-
raising in which all the surrounding neighbors participated. In

[5] Richmond, Robert and Mardock, Robert, *A Nation Moving West*,
pp. 24–6. (By permission of University of Nebraska Press, © 1966.)

most cases, the owner of the prospective cabin had cut the ash, beech or maple logs to the proper size and dragged them to the site. The workers, then assembled, would level the ground, notch the logs, split puncheons, chink the walls, make window frames and chimney slats. With all the logs in place, the door and window had to be cut out; since they were not built in as the cabin was raised. This heavy work was rushed to completion, according to Buley, "under the inspiration of liberal drafts of hard liquor and anticipation of sporting and gastronomic feats to come." Though primitive in their appearance, these log cabins inspired one author to write:

> . . . rude tenements, taunted and jeered at by an aristocratic party—yet still the citadels of our young republic—the low but mighty towers of our nation . . . .[6]

The furniture and household utensils were made from what the environment provided. A bed, for example, was constructed by placing two poles in the floor near one corner of the cabin. Rails were then attached from the poles to the cabin wall. The bed springs were fashioned from strands of rope, strips of deer hide or strings of twisted elm bark on top of which was placed a mattress of bearskins, cornhusks or feathers. Nearly every cabin had a sturdy old hickory broom and many of the eating utensils were made from the durable exterior of gourds.

The most useful and universal of all frontier tools was the ax. With it the pioneer settler built his cabin, cleared his land, fashioned crude furniture, hacked out farm implements, wooden utensils, and, according to Ray Billington, "edged her up a bit and shaved with her" on rare festive occasions. The research of R. C. Buley revealed the ax to be the favorite topic of frontier discussion. The fact that great pride was taken in the adeptness of its use (second only to skill in

[6] Buley, *op. cit.*, p. 144.

marksmanship); that a man would travel one hundred miles to secure the ax of his choice; and that the variety of styles was so large (Baltimore pattern, Yankee, single or double-bitted, concave or ridged, jumped, new-patent or homemade, double-portioned, light or heavy—to name a few) caused the subject of the ax to be more frequently and fully discussed than either politics or religion.

The first settlers in the Old Northwest bringing their traps and flintlocks found an abundance of food in the form of deer, bear, squirrel, ducks, geese, partridge, quail, pigeons and wild turkey. A week's supply of game food could be easily accumulated in half a day. In the nearby streams, they would seine and gig barrels full of wall-eyed pike and bass. Most of the settlers brought with them a cow which provided milk and the ingredients for butter and cheese. In addition, they usually planted their own vegetable patch which contained plenty of corn, pumpkin, beans and potatoes. The discovery of a hive filled with wild honey was considered the most valuable of finds. Salt was perhaps the most scarce of all necessary commodities. After discovering a salt-lick, the pioneer woman would have to boil approximately one hundred gallons of water in order to accumulate one bushel of salt.

The activities of frontier life were endless and varied, yet they followed something of a prescribed pattern from season to season. Spring was the time for plowing the fields, sowing the crops, planting a garden and—as the sap was beginning to rise—it was the perfect time for making maple sugar and syrup. In the early summer the crops had to be cultivated and by the late summer it was time for the harvest. The fall of the year brought a flurry of activity including corn husking, soap and candle making, butchering and the annual preparation of cider and apple butter. In their spare time they hunted game, split firewood, added an extra room or porch to the cabin, made their own clothes, canned fruits and vegetables, and repaired all of their farm implements.

In addition to the normal routine there were other challenges, such as protecting themselves from a variety of illnesses and from Indians, challenges which did not necessarily follow the seasons, but instead were among the settler's constant frontier companions. The Indian leaders of the Old Northwest, including Black Hawk and Red Bird, had been crowded from their land and aggravated beyond peaceful recourse. Consequently, they posed a continual threat.

It would constitute a physical impossibility to present a detailed description of every hardship, every chore, every danger and every annoyance with which the pioneer settler was forced to grapple. But perhaps the discussion of one tiny problem would serve to magnify the more serious hardships. Consider, then, R. C. Buley's very vivid description of the most common of pests—the housefly.

> Screens were lacking, manure piles were plentiful, and soon after settlements developed in any region, the housefly became a pest to be taken for granted. Swarms of them infested the cow barn or milk house, got into the milk and cream and even the butter. They overran the kitchen and filled the house. Dried fruit was frequently so bespecked as to be almost black. At mealtimes a fly switch of branches and leaves or a duster of narrow-cut paper strips was kept at hand to enable one of the children to "mind the flies." Babies slept with clusters of flies parading over their mouths. A few fastidious persons used cheese cloth or netting for protection, but flies were commonly accepted and regarded as much less dangerous than the night air. As a traveler described the situation during the summer:
>
> > The house is no sooner entered than you hear a continued hum, and the room is almost darkened by myriads of houseflies, which, in Illinois, are never seen out of doors, and which, when there are sick people in bed, require the constant atten-

tion of some assistant to drive them off, otherwise, if the patient were a child, or very weak, I believe they would soon suffocate him. Molasses, sugar, preserved fruit, bread, everything on the table, is loaded with them, and the very operation of fanning them off drives numbers of them into the molasses and other things of an adhesive nature. It is not safe to open your mouth. It is evident, too, on examining the molasses, that the small red ant has been purloining it, and has left a number of his unfortunate companions enveloped in its mass; whilst ever and anon a cockroach makes a dash at the table, and in nine cases out of ten, succeeds in scampering across over meat dishes and everything that comes in the way, and that too in spite of the bitter blows aimed at him with knife and spoon, he is "so t'nation spry." [7]

The Northwestern pioneer's own concept of his struggle for existence was often romanticized. In reminiscing about "the good old days," they often glossed over the solitude, savageness, ignorance, vulgarity, primitiveness and other major defects of frontier life. Said one old pioneer:

I recall my pioneer days as the happiest of my life. Coarse food and rough diet were the regimen of those days, but every cabin was a tent of refuge and relief from want. There were no instances of heaped up wealth, or pauper tramps. There existed . . . a general spirit of charity and free giving . . . . The condition of oppression and want was but the occasional tares in a general harvest of sweet anticipations, ever existing pleasure and happiness.[8]

[7] Buley, *op. cit.,* pp. 233–4.
[8] Buley, *op. cit.,* p. 139.

It should be noted that exaggeration in the reverse was also true. Many an old pioneer became overenthusiastic in describing his hardships and his fight for survival.

The Oregon Trail

As the pioneer settler discovered that the "old" Northwest and the Mississippi Valley were becoming crowded, he pressed further westward—in search of new trails, new lands and new opportunities. While treaties and battles were capturing the headlines of history, it was in this epic westward movement of the American people to settle half a continent that we find one of the most important dramas of the century. The poor, the oppressed, the ambitious, the adventurous—*together* they were attracted to the endless stretches of Western wilderness; and as a result, the "manifest destiny" of the nation to extend from the Atlantic to the Pacific was accomplished by the year 1860.

Identifying the new areas of settlement and describing the people who pioneered those regions has been skillfully accomplished by Ray Billington in *Westward Expansion* (p. 466).

> The pioneer farmers who followed the traders into the far west came largely from the Mississippi Valley frontier. There, in the tier of states bordering the Father of Waters, lived a hardier crew of frontiersmen than could be found elsewhere in the United States. Rich in experience but poor in cash, toughened by a rough-and-tumble environment where each man's revolver or bowie knife made the law, indoctrinated with a restlessness inherited from generations if pioneering forefathers, they made ideal colonizers. Between 1825 and 1845 they elbowed their way into Texas, peopled the lush valleys of Oregon, settled the forbidding wastes of the Great Basin, and

muscled into Spanish California in such numbers
the Mexican War only climaxed an annexation
movement well under way.

A combination of factors conspired to bring about the great
emigration to Oregon. A prolonged period of hard times
following the panic of 1837, a flood of alluring propaganda
in the form of exaggerated travelers' descriptions of the
Willamette Valley—journals of overenthusiastic trappers—
encouraging reports circulated by the federal government,
higher prices for farm produce and more favorable Pacific
markets—all of these tended to draw men in the direction
of the Columbia River.

An investigation of the westward movement of the pioneer
settler over the Oregon Trail reveals, among other things, the
physical environment of the West, the diverse types of people
who settled there, and the alternating impact of heritage and
environment. Jesse Applegate, an emigrant who endured the
hardships of trail life, remarked of his fellow travelers:

> . . . . No other race of men with the means at their
> command would undertake so great a journey,
> none save these could successfully perform it,
> with no previous preparation, relying only on the
> fertility of their own invention to devise the means
> to overcome each danger and difficulty as it arose.
> They have undertaken to perform with slowmoving
> oxen a journey of two thousand miles. The way
> lies over trackless wastes, wide and deep rivers,
> ragged and lofty mountains, and is beset with
> hostile savages. Yet, whether it were a deep river
> with no tree upon its banks, a rugged defile where
> even a loose horse could not pass, a hill too steep
> for him to climb, or a threatened attack of an
> enemy, they are always found ready and equal to
> the occasion, and always conquerors. May we not
> call them men of destiny? They are people
> changed in no essential particulars from their

> ancestors, who have followed closely on the foot-
> steps of the receding savage, from the Atlantic
> seaboard to the great Valley of the Missis-
> sippi . . . .[9]

Frederick Jackson Turner was in perfect agreement.

The great migration began with a flood of westward-bound emigrants converging on the frontier village of Independence, Missouri—the eastern terminus of the Santa Fe and Oregon Trails. During the month of May, the wagons and people assembled for the overland trek at this widely known center of trade. The pioneer's first encounter with Independence was a "Violent shock of strangeness"—a primary condition of the entire emigration. The historian, Bernard DeVoto, described the village best:

> All conditions of mankind were there, in all
> costumes: Shawnee and Kansa from the Territory
> and wanderers of other tribes, blanketed, painted,
> wearing their Presidential medals; Mexicans in
> bells, slashed pantaloons, and primary colors
> speaking a strange tongue and smoking shuck-
> rolled cigarettes; mountain men in buckskins pre-
> paring for the summer trade or offering their serv-
> ices to the emigrant trains; the case-hardened
> bull-whackers of the Santa Fe trail in boots and
> bowie knives, coming in after wintering at the
> other end or preparing to go out; riverman and
> roustabouts, Negro stevedores, soldiers from Fort
> Leavenworth, a miscellany of transients . . . .
>
> From now on the habits within whose net a man
> lives would be twisted apart and disrupted, and
> the most powerful tension of pioneering began
> here at the jumping-off. Here was a confusion of
> tongues, a multitude of strange businesses, a horde
> of strangers—and beyond was the unknown
> hazard. For all their exuberance and expectation,

[9] Hine and Bingham, *Frontier Experience,* p. 99.

160

doubt of that unknown fermented in the movers and they were already bewildered. They moved gaping from wheelwright's to blacksmiths, from tavern to outfitter's, harassed by drovers and merchants trying to sell them equipment, derided by the freighters, oppressed by homesickness, drinking too much forty-rod, forming combinations and breaking them up, fighting a good deal, raging at the rain and spongy earth, most of them depressed, some of them giving up and going ingloriously home.[10]

One traveler described Independence as a "great Babel upon the border of the wilderness." A more famous traveler, Francis Parkman, recorded his impressions of the wild and enterprising town in 1846.

The town was crowded. A multitude of shops had sprung up to furnish the emigrants and Santa Fe traders with necessaries for their journey; and there was an incessant hammering and banging from a dozen blacksmiths' sheds, where the heavy wagons were being repaired, and the horse and oxen shod. The streets were thronged with men, horses and mules.[11]

In this frontier urban environment, described by Parkman and DeVoto, the hardy pioneer made final preparations for his westward journey. Because supplies were available at only two or three forts along the way, each family had to buy enough provisions in Independence to last several weeks, perhaps even months. Careful consideration was given to both the cost and weight of supplies because the normal emigrant wagon had a capacity of only two to three thousand pounds. An average wagon load included the following items:

[10] DeVoto, *The Year of Decision—1846,* pp. 141–2.
[11] Parkman, *The Oregon Trail,* p. 16.

Food For One	Utensils	Spare Parts
Bacon —150 lbs.	2 Iron Kettles	Chain Links
Coffee — 25 lbs.	Frying Pan	Doubletrees &
Flour — 15 lbs.	Coffee pot	whippletrees
Sugar — 25 lbs.	Bake pan	Ox Yoke
Salt	Butcher knives	Harness parts
Pepper	Knives, forks,	Horseshoes & Ox
Saleratus (baking	spoons, Cups	shoes
soda)	Gutta-percha bucket	Tar bucket of grease
Beans and Rice	Medicines	Rope
Vinegar & Spices	Matches	Nails
	Soap	Buckskin
	Spade, Ax, Hammer	Ammunition
	Rifle and Revolver	Trinkets for Indians
		(Mirrors, Ribbons,
		Tobacco, etc.) [12]

One of the most important responsibilities of the westward-bound emigrant was his purchase of high quality stock to pull his wagon to Oregon. Although slower than mules, oxen were most frequently selected because they were less expensive, more durable, and not desired by the Indians. Young stock, which had been acclimated by at least a year's residence in the plains environment was the most preferable. The typical emigrant purchase was three or four yoke of oxen at $25 to $50 per span. The freight wagons traveling the Sante Fe Trail were much larger—with capacities of two to five tons—and required anywhere from five to ten yoke of oxen to pull the load. Even though they were cautious about such purchases, many emigrants were victimized with "bad stock" which died during the early weeks of the trip.

Although the average train consisted of approximately sixty wagons, it could range from twenty-five to well over one hundred. The wagons varied widely in size and sported a large assortment of different colored canvas tops. The average train of sixty wagons housed a cosmopolitan mixture

[12] Coons, Frederica, *The Trail to Oregon,* pp. 6–7, Binsford and Mort, Portland, Ore. (By permission of the author.)

of upwards from two hundred men, women and children. Opinion is mixed on the character of the emigrants. Francis Parkman, one of the best known contemporary observers, was very harsh in his judgment.

> Among them are some of the vilest outcasts in the country. I have often perplexed myself to divine the various motives that give impulse to this strange migration; but whatever they may be, whether an insane hope of a better condition in life, or a desire of shaking off restraints of law and society, or mere restlessness, certain it is that multitudes bitterly repent the journey, and after they have reached the land of promise are happy enough to escape from it.[13]

A less famous observer from Virginia with a much different perspective was far more complimentary when he noted that:

> The majority were plain, honest, substantial, intelligent, enterprising, virtuous . . . They were indeed much superior to those who usually settle in a new country.[14]

The migration was obviously heterogeneous, but the fact must be noted that it was far more difficult and expensive to make the 2000-mile trip from Missouri to Oregon than it had been to travel 500 miles from the eastern Piedmont into the Old Northwest. Many people simply could not afford the $1000 required to equip and supply themselves for the journey. "Moving West" was no longer the easiest recourse for those who had failed. The only way a very poor man could go was to hire on as a bullwhacker (wagon driver). Consequently, one might conclude that the Oregon migration was drawn from more stable elements than the previous migrations into the Old Northwest.

13 Parkman, *op. cit.*, p. 17.
14 DeVoto, *op. cit.*, p. 147.

The bulk of the emigrants were native American farmers who owned moderate amounts of property. In addition to American farmers, the wagon trains included people from nearly every country in northern Europe and representatives from all the major professions: lawyers, clergy, teachers, doctors, carpenters, blacksmiths, gunsmiths and stonemasons.

After purchasing their stock, repairing their wagons, securing the proper supplies, and dividing themselves into trains—the emigrant were still faced with the final chore of creating a suitable form of government before their departure. The process involved a considerable amount of electioneering before an acceptable set of rules could be adopted from the myriad of suggestions. They were free men on the move, taking the law with them and making it over to suit the needs of the day. Peter Burnett, an emigrant who traveled to Oregon in 1843, wrote the following account of the activity of organizing.

> The emigrants were from various places, unacquainted with each other, and there were among them many persons emulous of distinction, and anxious to wear the honors of the company. A great difference of opinion existed as to the proper mode of organization, and many strange propositions were made. I was much amused at some of them . . . . A red-faced old gentleman from east Tennessee state, high up on Big Pidgeon, near Kit Bullard's Mill, whose name was Dulany, generally styled "Captain," most seriously proposed that the meeting should adopt the criminal laws of Missouri or Tennessee, for the government of the company. This proposition he supported by an able speech, and several speeches were made in reply. Some one privately suggested that we should also take along a penitentiary, if Captain Dulany's proposition should pass.[15]

[15] Hine and Bingham, *op. cit.*, p. 96.

Although the typical organization had a very impressive list of officers—including a captain, several vice-captains, judges, secretary, treasurer, and a variety of committees—their authority was entirely theoretical. The members of the train, nearly always, reserved the right to object and to debate. Consequently, few trains ever reached Oregon with the same officers and organization which they selected in Independence. Some captains of trains were good, some poor, but most of them were average and learned as they drove.

Wagon Train Constitution

Resolved, Whereas we deem it necessary for the government of all societies, either civil or military, to adopt certain rules and regulations for their government, for the purpose of keeping good order and promoting civil and military discipline. In order to insure union and safety, we deem it necessary to adopt the following rules and regulations for the government of the said company:—

RULE 1. Every male person of the age of sixteen, or upward, shall be considered a legal voter in all affairs relating to the company.

RULE 2. There shall be nine men elected by a majority of the company, who shall form a council, whose duty it shall be to settle all disputes arising between individuals, and to try and pass sentence on all persons for any act for which they may be guilty, which is subversive of good order and military discipline. They shall take especial cognizance of all sentinels and members of the guard, who may be guilty of neglect of duty, or sleeping on post. Such persons shall be tried and sentence passed upon them at the discretion of the council. A majority of two thirds of the council shall decide all questions that If the captain disapprove of the decision of the council, he shall state to them his reasons, when they shall again pass upon the question, and if the same decision is again made by the same majority, it shall be final.

RULE 3. There shall be a captain elected who shall have supreme military command of the company. It shall be the duty of the captain to maintain good order and strict discipline, and as far as practicable, to enforce all rules and regulations adopted by the company. Any man who shall be guilty of disobedience of orders shall be tried and sentenced at the discretion of the council, which may extend to expulsion from the company. The captain shall appoint the necessary number of duty sergeants, one of whom shall take charge of every guard, and who shall hold their offices at the pleasure of the captain.

RULE 4. There shall be an orderly sergeant elected by the company, whose duty it shall be to keep a regular roll, arranged in alphabetical order, of every person subject to guard duty in the company; and shall make out his guard details by commencing at the top of the roll and proceeding to the bottom, thus giving every man an equal tour of guard duty. He shall also give the member of every guard notice when he is detailed for duty. He shall also parade every guard, call the roll, and inspect the same at the time of mounting. He shall also visit the guard at least once every night, and see that the guard are doing strict military duty, and may at any time give them the necessary instructions respecting their duty, and shall regularly make report to the captain every morning, and be considered second in command.

RULE 5. The captain, orderly sergeant, and members of the council shall hold their offices at the pleasure of the company, and it shall be the duty of the council, upon the application of one third or more of the company, to order a new election for either captain, orderly sergeant, or new member or members of the council, or for all of them, as the case may be.

RULE 6. The election of officers shall not take place until the company meet at Kansas River.

RULE 7. No family shall be allowed to take more than three loose cattle to every male member of the family of the age of sixteen and upward.[16]

At last the trains were prepared to begin their arduous journey. An early departure was essential—usually April, May or as soon as the grass began to turn green. The later a train left, the more probable was the hazard of a diminished supply of grass for the stock. It was also important that they leave soon enough to insure a safe crossing of the mountains before snowfall.

The objective of the first day on the trail was simply to ferry across the Missouri River, if they started from "St. Joe," or travel five to ten miles on to the prairie if they started from Independence.

Accounts differ in regard to the trail discipline which the emigrants imposed upon themselves. The historian, Bernard DeVoto, drew very critical conclusions, identifying the travelers on the Oregon Trail as "an uncohesive assemblage of individualists." He pointed to the near military discipline of the freight caravans on the Santa Fe Trail—traveling in columns of two or four and their systematized routine of travel and camp—as a striking contrast to emigrant travel on the Oregon Trail. Said DeVoto of the trail life to Oregon:

> . . . A captain who wanted to camp here rather than there had to make his point by parliamentary procedure and the art of oratory. It remained the precious right of a free American who could always quit his job if he didn't like the boss, to camp somewhere else at his whim or pleasure— and to establish his priority with his fists if some

[16] *Ibid.,* pp. 97–8.

other freeborn American happened to like the cottonwood where he had parked his wagon. Moreover, why should anyone take his appointed dust when he could turn off the trail? Why should he stand guard on the herd of loose cattle, if he had no cattle in it? . . . . They combined readily but with little cohesiveness and subdued themselves to the necessities of travel only after disasters had schooled them. They strung out along the trail aimlessly, at senseless intervals and over as wide a space as the country permitted. So they traveled fewer miles in any day than they might have, traveled them with greater difficulty than they needed to, and wore themselves and the stock down more than was wise. They formed the corral badly, with too great labor and loss of time, or not at all. They quarreled over place and precedence that did not matter. They postponed decisions in order to debate and air the minority view, when they should have accepted any decision that could be acted on. Ready enough to help one another through any emergency or difficulty, they were unwilling to discipline themselves to an orderly and sensible routine.[17]

Jesse Applegate, perhaps the most often quoted authority on the Oregon Trail, recalled his experiences as a member of one of the earliest wagon trains to cross the continent. His classic account offers an interesting contrast to DeVoto, but it should be noted that Applegate was reminiscing thirty-three years after the trip. Even so, Applegate's comments are valuable not only for their description of trail discipline and the character of the people, but also because they reveal the daily routine of trail life.

The migration of a large body of men, women and children across the continent to Oregon was,

[17] DeVoto, *op. cit.*, p. 154.

168

in the year 1843, strictly an experiment; not only in respect to the members, but to the outfit of the migrating party . . . . It is four o'clock A.M.; the sentinels on duty have discharged their rifles—the signal that the hours of sleep are over—and every wagon and tent is pouring forth its night tenants, and slow-kindling smoke begin largely to rise and float away in the morning air . . . by 5 o'clock the herders begin to contract the great, moving circle, and the well-trained animals move slowly towards camp, clipping here and there a thistle or a tempting bunch of grass on the way. In about an hour five thousand animals are close up to the encampment, and the teamsters are busy selecting their teams and driving them inside the corral to be yoked. The corral is a circle one hundred yeards deep, formed with wagons connected strongly with each other; the wagon in the rear being connected with the wagon in front by its tongue and ox chains . . . .

. . . From 6 to 7 o'clock is a busy time: breakfast is to be eaten, the tents struck, the wagons loaded and the teams yoked and brought up in readiness to be attached to their respective wagons. All know when, at 7 o'clock, the signal to march sounds, that those not ready to take their proper places in the line of march must fall into the dusty rear for the day.

There are sixty wagons. They have been divided into fifteen divisions or platoons of four wagons each, and each platoon is entitled to lead in its turn. The leading platoon today will be the rear one tomorrow . . . .

It is on the stroke of seven; the rush to and fro, the cracking of whips, the loud command to oxen, and what seemed to be the inextricable confusion of the last ten minutes has ceased. The clear notes of a trumpet sound in the front; the pilot and his guards mount their horses; the leading divisions of the wagons move out of the encampment, and

169

take up the line of march; the rest fall into their places with the precision of clock work, until the spot so lately full of life sinks back into that solitude that seems to reign over the broad plain . . . . The wagons form a line three quarters of a mile in length; some of the teamsters ride upon the front of their wagons, some walk beside their teams; scattered along the line companies of women and children are taking exercise on foot. The pilot, by measuring the ground and timing the speed of the wagons and the walk of the horses, has determined the rate of each, so as to enable him to select the nooning place, as nearly as the requisite grass and water can be had at the end of five hours' travel of the wagons . . . he and his pioneers are at the nooning place an hour in advance of the wagons, which time is spent in preparing convenient watering places for the animals . . . as the teams are not unyoked, but simply turned loose from the wagons, a corral is not formed at noon, but the wagons are drawn up in columns, four abreast the leading wagon of each platoon on the left . . . .

Today an extra session of the council is being held to settle a dispute . . . . It is now one o'clock; the bugle has sounded and the caravan has resumed its westward journey. It is in the same order, but the evening is far less animated than the morning march; a drowsiness has fallen apparently on man and beast; teamsters drop asleep on their perches and even when walking by their teams, and the words of command are now addressed to the slowly creeping oxen in the soft tenor of women or the piping treble of children, while the snores of the teamsters make a droning accompaniment . . . . the sun is now getting low in the west and at length the painstaking pilot is standing ready to conduct the train in the circle which he has previously measured and marked out, which is to form the invariable fortification for the night . . . . Within ten minutes from the time the leading wagon halted, the barricade is formed, the teams unyoked and driven out to pasture. Every one is busy preparing fires of buffalo chips to cook the evening meal, pitching tents and otherwise preparing for the night . . . . All able to bear arms in the party have been formed into three companies, and each of these into four watches; every third night it is the duty of one of these companies to keep watch and ward over the camp, and it is so arranged that each watch takes its turn of guard duty through the different watches of the night . . . . They begin at 8 o'clock P.M., and end at 4 o'clock A.M. meal is just over, and the corral now free from the intrusion of cattle or horses, groups of children are scattered over it . . . . Before a tent near the river a violin makes lively music, and some youths and maidens have improvised a dance upon the green . . . . It has been a prosperous day; more than twenty miles have been accomplished of the great journey . . . . But time passes; the watch is set for the night, the council of old men has broken up and each has returned to his own quarters . . . the violin is silent and the dancers have dispersed . . . . All is hushed and repose from the fatigue of the day . . . .[18]

Perhaps the organization of daily activities was not as exact as Applegate suggests, but nevertheless a certain routine was repeated day after day throughout 2,000 miles of alien and hostile land. The trail which covered this vast distance was so vaguely marked in some places that only experienced guides could lead the settlers through. After a few trains had made the trip, however, it was very clearly, and often, very grimly marked.

The people who traveled the road knew it by many names —the California Trail, the Platte Trail, the Mormon Trail, and the Oregon Trail. The Indians referred to it as the "Great

[18] Hine and Bingham, op. cit., pp. 98–103.

Medicine Road of the Whites" and the "White-topped Wagon Road."

The Oregon Trail followed the line of least resistance, staying close to creeks and rivers to assure the travelers of grass and water. Oxen pulled the wagons along this trail at a rate of two miles per hour. Depending on a wide variety of hazards, a wagon train traveled anywhere from ten to twenty miles per day.

From Independence to a point forty miles west, the Santa Fe and Oregon Trails followed the same route, moving along the south bank of the Kansas River, passing through the Shawnee Mission and finally arriving at the trails' junction marked with the famous sign, "Road to Oregon." The trail crossed the Kansas River at Papan's Ferry and continued northwest past Fort Leavenworth and on to Alcove Springs.

> About three-fourths of a mile from our camp we found a large spring of water . . . . Altogether it is one of the most romantic spots I ever saw . . . .
> We named this the "Alcove Spring"; and future travelers will find the name graven on the rocks . . . .
> 1846—Edwin Bryant[19]

At Alcove Springs, the emigrants were near the fording area on the Big Blue River, 175 miles from Independence. If rivers were too deep to ford, the settlers would build a crude raft from nearby cottonwoods and put it back and forth across the stream. Timber not being available, the travelers simply filled the cracks in the wagon box and used it as a boat. The stock had to swim across.

After crossing the Big Blue at Alcove Springs, the trail angled northwest along the Valley of the Little Blue, into "Newbrasky," eventually reaching Fort Kearney. At Fort Kearney, where the Mormon and Oregon Trails united, the emigrants were 300 miles from Independence and in need of

[19] Coons, *op. cit.,* pp. 41–2.

fresh supplies. Several travelers had already made the unfortunate discovery that merchants in Independence sold them supplies of inferior quality. One traveler noted:

> We discovered that we had been imposed upon . . .
> in the purchase of our bacon, for it began to exhibit more signs of life than we had bargained for.
> It became necessary to scrape and smoke it, in order to get rid of its tendency to walk in insect form.[20]

From Fort Kearney west the trail followed the Valley of the Platte for nearly 1,000 miles. The travelers had long and anxiously awaited their first view of the great river, but upon sighting it they were not always impressed. Francis Parkman remarked:

> At length . . . the long expected Valley of the
> Platte lay before us. We all drew rein, and sat
> joyfully looking down upon the prospect. It was
> right welcome; strange, too, and striking to the
> imagination, and yet it had not one picturesque
> or beautiful feature; nor had it any of the features
> of grandeur, other than its vast extent, its solitude,
> and its wildness . . . here and there, the Platte,
> divided into a dozen thread-like slices . . . and an
> occasional clump of wood, rising in the midst like
> a shadowy island . . . . It's low banks, for the most
> part without a bush or a tree, are of loose sand,
> with which the stream is so charged that it grates
> on the teeth in drinking . . . .[21]

By the time they reached Fort Kearney, the emigrants were gradually becoming more accustomed to trail life; but trail life became gradually more difficult to endure. The climate, consisting of heat waves, violent thunderstorms and northerly

[20] *Ibid.*, p. 18.
[21] Parkman, *op. cit.*, pp. 55–6.

winds of exceptional velocity, was almost intolerable. One settler remarked:

> Oxen might die of heat beside streams made impassable by yesterday's rain while the owner sniffed from a cold produced by day before yesterday's norther.[22]

Sudden and prolonged gusts of wind would flatten the tents and wagons, as well as produce a dust storm so severe that when it ended, people were unrecognizable—many had choked to death. Such a storm was often followed by a torrential downpour which resulted in flooding conditions, stampeded stock and mired wagons.

The most constant of all weather elements was the heat. It cracked their lips, peeled their cheeks, and turned their skins almost black. The dry air would shrink the wagon wheels; and without warning, a spoke would pull out, a wheel would roll off, and the wagon stall. The same brittleness would cause a wagon tongue to snap in two, and the wrecked wagon had to be converted to a cart.

In addition to the natural hazard of weather, the emigrants were also in the country of the Pawnee, who were expert thieves and raiders. Young bucks, just for fun, would raid or stampede the cattle, scare the travelers at night, or drive a herd of buffalo right through a train. The settlers traveled in chronic fear of the Indian, rarely daring to straggle from their wagons. The Pawnee weren't always looking for fun—and often massacred a whole train.

The buffalo provided a menace to the trains. The herds were immense and could easily overrun a camp. One traveler reported:

> As the gathering cloud came nearer on the opposite side of the valley . . . the ground seemed to fairly tremble . . . when a gust of wind from down

[22] DeVoto, *op. cit.,* p. 144.

river lifted the cloud for awhile, and we beheld a
compact black mass, extending beyond farther
than we could see and coming in unbroken masses
from the rear. The quaking of the earth and the
rumble of the torrent continued for a long time,
many estimating the herd to be from four to eight
miles long and of unknown width. Surely many,
many thousands of those animals.[23]

One wagon train was held up from before noon until sun-
down while such a herd crossed in front of them. Yet, there
were compensations. The buffalo was a source of fresh meat
and dried "jerky." The hide gave the travelers warm blankets,
and the dried manure or buffalo chips provided "prairie coal"
for the campfires.

Other than the buffalo, wild game food was somewhat
scarce, consisting of prairie chickens, jackrabbits, wild turkey
and perhaps a coyote or rattlesnake. Due to poor diets, bad
cooking, dirty utensils, poorly kept food and impure drinking
water, repeated epidemics of dysentery and diarrhea besieged
the trains. The most dreaded of trail diseases was cholera.
In the year 1852 alone, it took the lives of 5,000 emigrants
along the trail. Regardless of the year, everyone who kept a
diary noted the abundance of fresh graves. One woman com-
piled the following list through eight days of travel:

> June 14—passed seven new-made graves.
> 16—passed eleven new graves.
> 17—passed six new graves.
> 18—we have passed twenty-one new graves
> today.
> 19—passed thirteen graves today.
> 20—passed ten graves.
> 22—passed seven graves. If we should go
> by the camping grounds, we should see
> five times as many graves as we do.[24]

[23] Coons, *op. cit.*, p. 54.
[24] *Ibid.*, p. 50.

175

At the junction of the North and South Platte Rivers, the emigrants were faced with the decision of fording the river at that point, traveling another sixty miles southwest to an alternate crossing, or traveling yet another twenty miles to the Julesburg or Upper California crossing.

No matter the choice, the crossing was always dangerous. Quicksand, swift currents, mired stock—combating these along with other hazards required from one to two hours to take a single wagon across.

In western Nebraska, the trail brought the settlers to Ash Hollow—a real test of their ingenuity. Surrounded by high hills, the wagons had to be let down into the hollow by use of a "windless." Once into the hollow, it was the most pleasant camping area since they left Alcove Springs.

Beyond was alkali country where sudden gales of wind produced blindness in both men and their stock. Most water holes were dry; those that weren't held water that was unfit to drink. Oxen bloated on the foul water, their hooves swelled and festered in the alkali and rocks; and as the grass diminished, many grew gaunt and died.

Withstanding the endless hardships, the process of life— marriage, birth, and death continued as the wagons crossed the plains. DeVoto described it best.

> The guests formed a procession behind a fiddler and conducted Mr. and Mrs. Mootrey to the nuptial tent. A mile away they saw faint sparks moving by twos in another procession, torches lighting the dead boy's body to its desert grave. A mile or so in the opposite direction still a third train was camped, and there at the same moment a dozen desert-worn women were ministering to one of their sisterhood who writhed and screamed under a dusty wagon cover . . . and in due time her child was born.[25]

As the wagons moved westward the loads seemed heavier

[25] DeVoto, *op. cit.*, p. 163.

and the distance they traveled in a day was shortened. Consequently the settlers began disposing of excess weight, and the trail became strewn with ornate pieces of furniture, ancestral relics, household goods and a variety of utensils. The trail litter represented not only the folly of the emigrants as their journey began, but more important, it represented a portion of their family heritage which an overpowering environment dictated they leave behind. The immediate effects of the trail environment often left an indelible imprint upon the travelers.

> . . . Drenched blankets, cold breakfasts after rainy nights, long hours without water, exhaustion from the labor of double-teaming through a swamp or across quicksands or up a slope, from ferrying a swollen river till midnight, from being roused to chase a strayed ox across the prairie two hours before dawn, from constant shifting of the load to make the going better. Add the ordinary hazards of the day's march: a sick ox, a balky mule, the snapping of a wagon tongue, capsizing at a ford or overturning on a slope, the endless necessity of helping others who had fallen . . . . Add the endless apprehension about your stock, the ox which might die, every days threat that the animals on which your travel depended might be killed by disease or accident or Indians, leaving you stranded in the waste, Such things worked a constant attrition on the nerves . . . add to them a bad storm or some neighbor's obstinacy that reacted to the common loss. The sunniest grew surly and any pinprick could be a mortal insult. The enforced companionship of the trail began to breed hatred . . . . The very width and openness of the country was an anxiety . . . the strongest personality diminished. There was no place to hide in, and always there was the sun to hide from . . . the little line of wagons was pygmy motion in immensity, the mind became a speck. A speck always quivering with an unidenti-

fied dread which few could face and which the
weaker ones could not control. The elements of
human personality were under pressure . . . . Some
survived it unchanged or strengthened in their
identity; some suffered from it, inflicting it on their
families, for the rest of their lives. And it grew
as the trip went on. Worse country lay ahead and
the drained mind was less able to meet it.[26]

At intervals between Ash Hollow and Scotts Bluff, a number
of enormous rock formations, identified by one author as
nature's slag heap, marked the trail. The first of these formations was named Jail and Courthouse Rocks. But perhaps
the most famous of all landmarks along the trail was Chimney
Rock.

> . . . at this place was a singular phenomenon,
> which is among the curiosities of the country. It
> is called the Chimney. The lower part is a conical
> mound rising out of the naked plain; from the
> summit shoots up a shaft or column, about one
> hundred and twenty feet in height, from which it
> derives its name. The height of the whole . . . is a
> hundred and seventy five yards . . . and may be
> seen at the distance of upwards of thirty miles.
> Capt. Benjamin Bonneville 1832 [27]

Though described by the famous, it is in the journals of
hundreds of covered wagon emigrants that Chimney Rock's
importance to the pioneers can best be gaged. From far out
on the plains, wagon-train scouts could see the spire. To
them it heralded progress and signaled that the second phase
of their long journey was about to begin. Although its chief
attraction was as an oddity, its main benefit was as a camp-
site with a nearby spring.

[26] *Ibid.*, pp. 159–60.
[27] U.S. Dept. of Interior, National Park Service, *Chimney Rock,*
pamphlet by U.S. Govt. Printing Office, 1966, p. 1.

From Chimney Rock, the earlier trains traveled through Robidoux Pass to miss the rugged bluffs near the river. Later trains, however, discovered a route through the bluffs and thereafter, Mitchell Pass or Scotts Bluff became the most popular crossing point. The trail from Mitchell Pass, all the way to Fort Laramie, followed along between bluffs on the south and the Platte River on the north.

Fort Laramie came as a welcome relief to the trail-weary travelers. These were the first buildings they had seen since leaving the Shawnee mission in eastern Kansas. At Fort Laramie the emigrants rested for a few days, . . . writing letters home, repairing their wagons, buying fresh supplies from Sutler's store, having their stock re-shod or in many cases trading their oxen for mules which were better for crossing the mountainous terrain that awaited them.

One day out of Fort Laramie, the emigrants camped at Registar Cliff where many of them carved their names for future travelers to read. The next important objective on the trail was an enormous rock, measuring one mile in circumference at its base, located in southcentral Wyoming. At that point the wagon trains were 838 miles from Independence, Missouri. They usually arrived at the rock in early July; and because so many of the trains camped near there on July 4, it was given the name, Independence Rock.

After carving their names into Independence Rock, the emigrants continued their journey across the Sweetwater River, passed Devil's Gate and on through South Pass. At South Pass they were just half way to Oregon and the worst part of the trip was still ahead of them.

The trail angled southwest from the pass and the travelers were faced with the decision of using the Sublette cut-off or going on south to Fort Bridger. Most of the travelers selected the latter route. The Donner party was among many, however, who chose the cut-off. At Fort Bridger, 1,070 miles from where they started, the emigrants stopped to replenish their supplies for the remainder of the trip. The fort was established in 1843 by the widely known trapper and trader, Jim Bridger; but it went out of business just ten years later.

> I have established a small fort with a blacksmith shop and a supply of iron in the road of the emigrants on Blacks Fork of Green River which promises fairly. They, in coming out, are generally well supplied with money, but by the time they get there are in want of all kinds of supplies. Horses, provisions, smith work, etc., bring ready cash from them, and should I receive the goods hereby ordered will do a considerable business in that way with them.[28]

From Fort Bridger, the trail turned north by the oasis of Soda Springs and then on to Fort Hall. There was an abundance of both water and grass on this section of the trail. It was also the section which contained various cut-off routes leading to the Humboldt River and on to California. Many emigrants made the decision to splinter off in that direction.

At Fort Hall the trail joined the Snake River and followed it for 300 miles all the way to Oregon. It was a barren stretch of land filled with stretches of sand, alkali, dust and wind. After leaving Fort Boise, near the Oregon border, the settlers had to cross the Blue Mountains to reach the Columbia River. This was one of the most treacherous parts of the trip, and the journey of fifty miles consumed four days of travel. Some of the emigrants went all the way to Fort Walla Walla while others chose the Umatilla cut-off.

Upon reaching the Columbia River, the remaining 300 miles was very often traveled in 40-foot long canoe-shaped boats called *bateaux*. In contrast to the slow moving wagon trains this last 300 miles by water required only five days of travel. Some of the settlers chose to finish the trip by wagon, rather than sell their remaining possessions at Fort Walla Walla and complete the trip to the Dallas.

[28] Coons, *op. cit.*, p. 114.

180

At last, in the month of October, the journey was ended. Although tired and strained after enduring the experiences of six months of trail life, the emigrants had to draw upon all of their ingenuity and heritage to adapt themselves to a new environment and create a civilized place to live. Most were optimistic:

> We . . . lost twenty head of cattle and four horses in getting to Oregon, which besides various other losses, would have brought us, Oregon prices about $1500. We hope, however, to soon make it up if health and life are spared . . . Country around presents some handsome scenery, as well as good soil. Well watered and covered with a luxurious growth of all wild products.[29]

. . . but some were very discouraged.

> If there are any persons in Sangamon who speak of crossing the Rocky Mountains to this country, tell them my advice is to stay at home. There you are well off. You can enjoy all the comforts of life—live under a good government and have peace and plenty around you—a country whose soil is not surpassed by any in the world, having good seasons and yielding timely crops. Here everything is on the other extreme: the government is tyrannical, the weather unseasonable, poor crops, and the necessaries of life not to be had except at the most extortionate prices, and frequently not then . . . .[30]

Settlement of the Great Plains

A map of the United States drawn in the mid-nineteenth century contained a space extending from the Missouri River to the Rocky Mountains and from the Texas Panhandle

[29] *Ibid.*, p. 160.
[30] DeVoto, *op. cit.*, p. 125.

to the Canadian border labeled the "Great American Desert." This area was legally opened to settlement by the passage of the bitterly debated Kansas–Nebraska Act in 1854; but the real settlement boom followed the enactment of the Homestead Act in 1862. Settlers moved to the plains by the hundreds, and the "farmer's frontier"—which had begun east of the Appalachian range a century before, extended into the Old Northwest, and then traveled the overland trail to the new Northwest—gradually began to fill the void it had passed over.

> The first permanent settlers on the prairies were those adventurous ones who feared neither the dangers of Indian attacks nor the privations of life in a region remote from civilization. They formed a frail, thin line of settlement along the overland trails . . . . This development was a new thing in the history of the frontier. It is true that settlement often followed rivers but never before had settlement pushed out across a barren area . . . .[31]

The Great Plains region presented an environment much different from previous frontiers. The blistering heat of summer and the raging blizzards of winter, the seasons of drought and the deluges of rain, the spring tornados and the breathless summer nights, together created an exhausting challenge.

The pioneers found very little that was familiar to them. Timber for homes, sheds or split-rail fences was almost nonexistent. There was seldom enough rainfall and consequently water had to be taken from deep wells, rather than a nearby stream. Normal farming operations were futile because of the tough prairie sod; and, in order to succeed, the frontiersman had to devise new methods or purchase newly developed farm implements. The human ingenuity required to conquer this strange environment produced innovations which

[31] Dick, Everett, *The Sod-House Frontier*, p. 102. (Courtesy Johnson Publishing Co., Lincoln, Neb., © 1954.)

were altogether strange to the traditional farmer—barbed wire, windmills and sod buildings.

As the farmer's frontier approached the fringes of the cattle kingdom, there was an increased demand for efficient fencing material. Farmers had to have fences of one kind or another to prevent livestock and trespassers from ruining their crops. The stone fences of New England had given way to rail fences in the Old Northwest; but the split-rail fence proved highly impractical on the Great Plains. A 160-acre homestead which cost its owner $20 in fees required $1,000 to fence, including both purchase and shipping costs.

Hundreds of inventors took out patents on new types of cheap fencing but one solution proved superior to all the rest. It was devised by Joseph Farwell Glidden, a farmer near DeKalb, Illinois. His new idea was best described by the historian Ray Allen Billington:

> Faced with the problem of enclosing his own six-hundred-acre farm, Glidden devised a practical fence by twisting together two strands of wire in such a way they would hold pointed wire barbs at short intervals. After convincing himself the "barbed wire" fence could be produced cheaply, he patented his invention on November 24, 1874, rented a small factory in De Kalb, hired a crew of boys to string the barbs on the twisted strands, and began manufacturing his product as the Barb Fence Company.[32]

Joseph Glidden was not the first person to design barbed wire, patents having been issued as early as 1801. The difference in Glidden's product was that it could be mass produced by using machines, thus making it available at a price most could afford. Nearly 3,000,000 pounds of barbed wire were sold in 1876 and by 1880 the figure had soared to 80,000,000 pounds. The price of the wire dropped from $20

[32] Billington, *Westward Expansion,* p. 691.

per hundred pounds in 1870 to less than $4 by 1890. Historian Walter Prescott Webb remarked:

> It was barbed wire, and not railroads or the homestead law that made it possible for the farmers to resume, or at least accelerate, their march across the prairies onto the plains . . . . The invention of barbed wire revolutionized land values and opened up to the homesteader the fertile Prairie Plains.[33]

The strongest resistance to barbed wire came from the cattle ranchers who had designated most of the territory between Texas and Wyoming as open range—unfenced. As the rangeland was gradually fenced off by nestors, the cattlemen considered themselves threatened with extinction. The cattle drovers referred to the new wire fencing as bob wire, the Devil's Rope, the Devil's Necklass or the Devil's Hatband. The drovers' hostility stemmed from such grievances as the sealing off of vital sources of water, stock continually injuring themselves on the wire, trails being blocked and cattle dying because fences prevented them from reaching shelter during blizzards. Many of the cattlemen resorted to wire cutting, a practice which resulted in what some historians have identified as the Barbed Wire War.

Water was as essential to plains agriculture as good fencing. The pioneers soon discovered that methods which had proven successful on earlier frontiers, such as the open well, were not usable on the Great Plains. Most settlers resorted to expensive well-drilling machines to reach the deep sub-surface pools. Well drillers charged from $1.25 to $2 a foot to drill a well which in the plains country could be anywhere from fifty to five-hundred feet. After reaching the water, they were still faced with the problem of raising it to the surface. With an average wind velocity of twelve to fourteen miles per hour sweeping the plains, the logical solution was to devise a windmill. The cost of a manufactured windmill ranged from $100 to $150; so many settlers decided to build their own.

[33] Webb, *Great Plains,* pp. 316–17.

Windmills varied in construction and appearance with the owner's imagination, skill and available building materials. The farmers gave descriptive names to their proud creations such as "jumbo," "go-devil," "battle-axe" or "merry-go-round." The prairie settlers found their materials for windmill construction in the gears, cogs and levers of broken-down farm machinery, scrap lumber, canvas from old tarpaulins, packing boxes and flattened tin cans. Homemade mills were an object of considerable pride. Walter Webb once made the observation that:

> The windmill is like a flag marking the spot where
> a small victory had been won in the fight for water
> in an arid land.[34]

Another pressing need of the hardy settler in his conquest of the prairie was adequate housing. Upon locating his homestead, the settler prepared a temporary shelter by excavating a dugout in the side of a hill or in a ravine. The family lived in the wagon box while the father used the running gears to haul brush, grass and sod.

An estimated cost of constructing a dugout fourteen foot square in 1872 was given by an old settler named Oscar Babcock.

One window	$1.25
18 feet of lumber for front door	.54
Latch and hanging (no lock)	.50
Length of pipe to go through roof	.30
3 lbs. nails to make door, etc.	.19½
Total	$2.78½ [35]

Months later, the pioneers would erect a more permanent structure called a sod house. The process of construction was

[34] Danker, Donald, "Nebraska's Homemade Windmills" *The American West,* Vol. III, #1, 1966, p. 15. (By permission of *The American West Magazine.*)

[35] Dick, *Sod-House Frontier,* p. 112.

interestingly described by Charles S. Reed, who helped build
several "soddies" as a young boy.

> The first step was to "break" the ground, which
> was done by turning the sod over with a "breaking
> plow" . . . . The moldboard of a breaking plow
> consisted of three curved rods that turned the sod
> over grass side down, instead of a solid metal
> plate . . . . Pieces of sod used in building were
> usually about three inches thick, twelve inches
> wide, and thirty inches long . . . .
>
> The mechanics of building a sod house were
> fairly simple, but required good workmanship to
> put up a good one . . . . The first tier of sod was
> laid grass side down on the virgin ground site.
> If the building space was not level, the lower
> corners were built up by sod so that the upper
> tiers of sod in the wall would be level . . . .
>
> In erecting a wall, the slabs of sod were criss-
> crossed so that the joints would be broken all the
> way up the wall. Thus each layer of sod (all of
> which were laid grass side down) was laid into the
> wall differently from the layer below it . . . .
>
> If you kept the walls straight, it was pretty easy
> going until you reached the top of an opening
> where a window or door was to be. A door open-
> ing was provided by just not laying any sod in the
> door area, and a window opening was provided by
> running the solid wall only up to the bottom of the
> window and then leaving an open area the size of
> a window. The top of a window or door opening
> required special care. It was necessary to place
> some flat boards across the top of the window or
> door opening to support the wall that had to be
> on top . . .
>
> The most important thing about a sod house was
> its roof. The common sod house had a gable roof
> . . . . In my country, getting a good ridge pole long
> enough to reach from the top of one outside end

wall to the other end of the house, or even to a sod cross partition, was quite a job. In the early days, such a piece of timber was . . . always a long tree trimmed down. If the builders were lucky enough to have flat boards, one end of the board was nailed to the top center of the ridge pole and then extended down over the side walls about two feet. Then paper (tar paper if they could afford it) was placed on top of the sheeting boards and then sod (grass side up) was closely fitted together so as to form a slanting roof down to the end of the eaves. This made as good a roof as you could build unless you could afford wooden shingles . . . .

Flooring varied. In most of the earliest soddies the ground on the inside of the house would be leveled and swept free of any dust, and then the hard dirt surface would be covered by homemade rag carpets or often used bare. Most of the sod houses I remember, however, had at least rough board floors.

Sometimes the interior would be just the plain ends of the sod smoothed off. However, most people tried to improve this, and would cover the inside walls with paper, cloth or plaster. The plaster . . . was a mixture of sand and clay troweled onto the sod wall . . . . People who were lucky enough to afford cement would put it into the plaster mix, and this made fairly permanent plaster. Generally speaking, the outside walls were left plain, but a few people plastered the outside. Some that could not afford to plaster the wall on the outside with cement would put a fine mesh wire over the outside walls.

Most people visualize life in a soddy as being very dirty, but actually a sod house could be kept quite clean. A good sod house was always comfortable . . . . Sod houses were durable too . . . .[36]

[36] From *A Nation Moving West* (pp. 306–8) by Robert Richmond and Robert Mardock. (By permission of University of Nebraska Press, © 1966.)

Life in a sod house wasn't always pleasant. During rainstorms, for example, the roof became soggy and rivulets of water dripped all over the house. The roof continued to drip for several days after the rain had ended, and the floor became a quagmire. Women recalled having an umbrella held over them while they cooked or were sick in bed. Occasionally, the whole roof would cave in from the excess weight of saturation. Even in dry weather, dirt and grass continually fell from the ceiling.

The sod house was not without its advantages. It was cool in summer, warm in winter, rarely blew over in the high winds and was in no danger of destruction by prairie fires. In addition, sod house construction was very inexpensive as attested to by Howard Ruede in 1877, a Kansas homesteader:

> . . . I made out an estimate of the cost of our house. This does not include what was paid for in work: Ridgepole and hauling (including two loads of firewood) $1.50; rafters and straw, 50¢; 2 lb. nails, 15¢; hinges 20¢; window 75¢; total cash paid $4.05. Then there was $4 worth of lumber, which was paid for in work, and $1.50 for hauling the firewood, 50¢, makes $10.05 for a place to live in and firewood enough to last all summer . . . .[37]

The average life of a sod house was six to seven years.

Plains Environment

Plains environment made life exceptionally difficult because every season brought new hardships. Winters could be especially severe with fierce blizzards and temperatures which remained below zero for weeks. Women's feet froze while doing normal household chores. Water would freeze in the glasses at mealtime. The fact that two to three inches of snow

[37] Ruede, *Sod House Days,* pp. 27, 29, 43.

blew through the cracks into a sod house in one night was considered normal. Hogs, cattle, chickens and horses were frequently moved into the one room soddies with the people for mutual survival. When fuel became scarce, they were forced to chop up their furniture to burn.

Raging spring floods added to the settler's hardships, especially among those who had settled near streams which appeared to be nearly dry in summer. In the spring, after the heavy snows began to melt, these dry streams swelled to a boiling menace, sweeping away houses, barns, fences, livestock, implements, and anything that stood in their path.

The summer months normally brought searing heat waves which parched the soil and burned the crops. For weeks at a time the temperature did not fall below 100 degrees. Although it wasn't a joking matter, many Plains pioneers often remarked in jest that sinners were buried in overcoats to protect them from sudden changes in temperature. The monotony of a summer heat was occasionally broken by a devastating tornado, a pounding hail storm or a choking dust storm.

From 1874 to 1877 the plainsmen, in addition to all other summer hardships, had to endure the grasshopper plagues. The insects appeared as enormous clouds and when they settled they pelted houses like hailstones and alighted on trees in such great numbers that their weight broke off large limbs. They ate everything—cornstalks, grain, garden vegetables underground, leaves and bark of trees, pitchfork and plow handles, lumber off of the houses, clothes, and even the horses' harness. When the insects left, the whole country was a scene of ruin and desolation. Many settlers were forced to accept relief from either the territorial or United States government. Others packed up what remained and left the Plains forever.

One of the greatest terrors of the Plains farmers was the prairie fire which occurred most frequently in autumn. A campfire, the discharge of a gun, a spark, a bolt of lightning— any one of these was enough to start a blaze in the dry fall grass, which moved across the plains destroying stock, stacks

189

of hay, winter range, barns and occasionally a human life. Fires often lasted as long as six weeks. Plains inhabitants who were accidentally caught in such a fire had to start a backfire or quickly get into a dugout in order to save their lives. The fire left a strange darkness, as reported by one Kansas pioneer:

> The darkness that follows the going out of a prairie fire is something portentous. From being the center of a lurid glare you are suddenly plunged into the bottom of a bucket of pitch. Nothing reflects any light, and there is nothing to steer by. You don't know where you are nor where the house is; everything is black. Your throat is full of ashes and you can hardly breathe .... You may feel as if you were the last survivor in a horrible world of cinders and blackness.[38]

Fuel was as difficult to acquire as water. Many of the pioneers depended upon dried buffalo chips or cow manure. In the fall of the year these were gathered by the wagonload and stacked up for winter. Fortunate indeed was a farmer when a trail drive bedded down for the night near his property, because he was given a winter's supply of fuel. As the herds of buffalo and cattle disappeared, the farmers used either the woody stalks of sunflowers or dry grass which they twisted. Special stoves called "Hay-Burners" were widely sold in the 1870's.

The Plains environment was especially unkind to the women. Many of them were accustomed to the more pleasant chores of housekeeping in the East. Some of them burst into tears at the first sight of their home, but others managed enough courage to stay. To the valor of these women, the historian, Everett Dick, paid high tribute:

> These solitary women, longing to catch a glimpse of one of their own sex, swept their eyes over the

[38] Dick, *Sod-House Frontier*, p. 219.

boundless prairie and thought of their old home in the East. They stared and stared out across space with nothing to halt their gaze over the monotonous expanse. Sometimes the burning prairie got to staring back at them and they lost their courage. They saw their complexion fade as the skin became dry and leathery in the continual wind. Their hair grew lifeless and dry, their shoulders early bent, and they became stooped as they tramped round and round the hot cookstove preparing the three regular, though skimpy meals a day. There was little incentive to primp and care for one's person. Few bothered much about brush and comb. Hollow-eyed, tired, and discouraged in the face of summer heat, drought, and poverty, they came to care little about how they looked. As has been noted some begged their husbands to hitch up the team, turn the wagon tongue eastward and leave the accursed plains, which they declared were never meant for human habitation.

But by no means were all the women crushed and defeated by the rude frontier. Many a member of the sunbonnet sex bore her loneliness, disappointment, and heartaches without a complaint, and encouraged her husband to stick it out in the face of failure, frustration, and utter rout. Valorously she rallied the broken forces and assailed the common enemy once more. Brushing aside the unbidden tears, she maintained her position by the side of her hardy helpmate, and together, unflinchingly they waged a winning struggle against the odds of poverty, defeat and loneliness.[39]

Frontier Customs

Life on the Plains was not entirely dismal. Although most of the prairie homesteaders bordered on being poverty-

[39] *Ibid.*, pp. 234–5.

stricken, they still maintained their hospitality and neighbor-liness, even to strangers. The Sunday visit was one of the most common social events on the prairie. Families would spend the entire day together, sharing food and conversation, all of which helped to dispel their loneliness.

Though careless in dress, crude in manners and coarse in language, the homesteaders held a loyal concern for each other. The very nature of the frontier created a community spirit. Neighbors frequently came together because of some-one's misfortune. They joined in the spring plowing, a house raising, or a husking bee. Regardless of sex or wealth every-one was treated with an equal respect; yet the laws governing marriage and divorce were exceptionally lax.

Dancing was perhaps the most enjoyed of all amusements. Any occasion warranted a dance—holidays, weddings, birth-days, the opening of a new store, or just celebrating the end of harvest. For the most part, dances were gala affairs even in the communities which were not fortunate enough to have musicians. Often, dances were held with only a single mouth harp providing the music. In Nebraska, a dance was re-ported in the local newspaper as having had a big drum, a little drum, a fiddle, a pitchfork for a triangle, a keg of beer for company, and considerable noise for variety. Masquerade and calico balls were very popular in the frontier towns. Several town councils proposed the construction of dancing schools before they did high schools.

For other types of social entertainment, the pioneers en-joyed playing an infinite variety of card games, checkers and dominoes. Fourth of July picnics and barbecues were also quite popular along with the sports of hunting, baseball, croquet, mumble peg, keno, wrestling, foot racing, marksman-ship, horse racing, broad jumping and high jumping. These sports, however, should not be thought of in modern terms. The high jump area consisted of a string held between two cornstalks or posts, while horse racing was usually a contest between two old plow horses. Baseball games were played without the assistance of backstops, masks or gloves. They used only a bat fashioned from a board or fence post and a ball made of a roll of yarn, twine or string which was covered with a piece of leather from an old boot. They played the game with two to four bases, depending on available materials. The game was filled with action and the scores were generally high. In 1871, the Milford, Nebraska, Blue Belts were leading in their game after four hours of play, by a score of 97 to 25.

Such things as a community raffle, a traveling revival, a medicine show or a circus occasionally broke the monotony of prairie life. For the most part, their entertainment was homemade.

When the homesteader spoke, he emitted a strange and gnarled dialect. Yet his speech was forthright and anyone who spoke differently was thought to be "puttin on." A sampling of their speech proves colorful.

Word	Prairie Dialect
Terrible	— Powerful Bad
Afternoon	— Eveni
Sunrise	— Sunup
Opportunity	— Right smart chance
Pail	— Bucket
Spider	— Skillet
Fifty cents	— Four bits
Whiskey	— Strychnine
Sickness	— Yaller behind the gills
Funeral	— A buryin

The settlers' diet was infrequently varied. Day after day the menu consisted only of corn. In 1862, the *Nebraska Farmer* published a list of thirty-three different recipes for cooking corn. The prairie environment contained few fruits, berries or wild game so most of the homesteaders were forced to rely upon the productivity of their own gardens.

There was a great informality in prairie government. The selection of a county seat often erupted into a "county seat war," between two centers which were hardly more than dry spots on the Plains. One writer reported such a war among three small Nebraska towns, all competing for the honor.

> Republican City and Melrose each had a store, hitching post, and a clothes line, while Alma had only her buffalo skull.[40]

Elections were very frequent and often very heated. They were usually held under a shade tree or in a settler's dugout. Voters were occasionally asked to line up behind their candidate and then file by to vote. After casting their votes, many returned to the line to vote again. One man was observed voting five times. When questioned, he replied that he voted once for himself and cast four proxy votes for his friends who would have voted for his candidate except they were out of the territory.

A meeting of the legislature was usually a very exciting affair. In 1862, the quarrels grew so violent in the Dakota legislature that the governor was forced to send an armed detachment of twenty cavalrymen with fixed bayonets into the House of Representatives to preserve order. During such meetings, members could be observed whittling, sleeping, sitting on top of their desks or just walking around. One man was seen eating hard boiled eggs with a jackknife. It was not at all uncommon to adjourn the meeting to a nearby saloon.

The political campaigns were equally exciting. In the midst of loud music, excessive drinking and violent fist fights, a candidate would mount a heap of barnyard refuse and deliver a fiery speech. Crude though they were, these were the beginnings of government on the Great Plains.

[40] *Ibid.*, p. 460.

Conclusion

Although the Plains environment bordered on the intolerable, settlers homesteaded there in unprecedented numbers. Ray Allen Billington reported that

> A larger domain was settled in the last three decades of the century than in all America's past; 407,000,000 acres were occupied and 189,000,000 improved between 1607 and 1870; 430,000,000 acres peopled and 225,000,000 placed under cultivation between 1870 and 1900. Surveying that breath-taking advance, the director of the census announced in 1890 that the country's "unsettled area has been so broken into by isolated bodies of settlement that there can hardly be said to be a frontier line." [41]

That settlers could succeed in the plains environment in such numbers was largely due to the inventive genius of such men as James Oliver and Cyrus McCormack. These men were representative of the inventors who produced the farm implements which conquered the plains—iron and steel plows, grain drills, reapers, disk and toothed harrows, cultivators, binders, listers, headers, threshing machines and combines.

To the Industrial Revolution the sod-house farmer owed a great indebtedness. In 1890, the United States Commissioner of Labor produced figures showing the savings in time and money for one acre of produce. The figures revealed a dramatic story.

[41] Billington, *Westward Expansion,* p. 705.

Crop	Time Worked		Labor Cost	
	Hand	Machine	Hand	Machine
Wheat	61 hours	3 hours	$3.55	$.0.66
Corn	39 hours	15 hours	3.62	1.51
Oats	66 hours	7 hours	3.73	1.07
Loose Hay	21 hours	4 hours	1.75	0.42
Baled Hay	35 hours	12 hours	3.06	1.29 [42]

In most cases, however, the farmer lost as much as he gained. A man could homestead on the plains for as little as the $10 filing fee and a promise to build a suitable habitation within a year. Many of the people who came had a very difficult time accumulating the necessary $10. Obviously, they couldn't begin to pay for expensive machinery, fencing material or drilling a well.

In addition, land speculators had created a fraud out of the Homestead Act. The small farmer who came west in the hope of getting a free homestead, often discovered that he had to accept inferior land because the speculators had consolidated the choice lands into tracts to be sold at exorbitant prices. Speculators accumulated the land by circumventing the requirement of a suitable habitation. Some built miniature houses while others rented portable cabins on wheels for $5. The system of inspection was totally inadequate and thousands of acres passed into the hands of speculators for 50¢ an acre, and was in turn sold to the farmers at a cost of $5 to $10 per acre.

Subjected to privations and an angry environment, indebted to the Industrial Revolution and in debt to the speculators, the sod-house farmer somehow withstood it all—and could even recall his experiences with a bit of pleasure. An old pioneer living in more recent times, recalled the days of settling and building the West. He thoughtfully remarked:

> By Damn, wouldn't it be fun to tear it down and
> start all over again! !

[42] *Ibid.,* p. 697.

Bibliography

The Old Northwest

Buley, R. C.	*The Old Northwest,* Vols. I & II Indiana University Press, Bloomington, Ind.	1950 ed.
Caruso, John	*The Great Lakes Frontier* Bobbs-Merrill, Indianapolis, Ind.	1961 ed.
Ellis, William	*The Cuyahoga* Holt, Rinehart, Winston, New York, N.Y.	1966 ed.
Havighurst, Walter	*The Heartland* Harper, New York, N.Y.	1956 ed.
James, Alfred	*The Ohio Company* University of Pittsburgh Press, Pittsburgh, Pa.	1959 ed.
Jones, Evan	*Citadel in the Wilderness* Coward-McCann, New York, N.Y.	1966 ed.
McKee, Russell	*Great Lakes Country* Thomas Y. Crowell, New York, N.Y.	1966 ed.
Sandburg, Carl	*Abraham Lincoln: The Prairie Years* Harcourt, Brace & World, New York, N.Y.	1926 ed.

The Oregon Trail

Coons, Frederica	*The Trail to Oregon* Binfords & Mort, Portland, Ore.	1954 ed.
DeVoto, Bernard	*The Year of Decision: 1846* Houghton-Mifflin, Cambridge, Mass.	1942 ed.
Ghent, William	*The Road to Oregon* Longmans, Green, New York, N.Y.	1929 ed.
Gregg, J. R.	*A History of the Oregon Trail* Binfords & Mort, Portland, Ore.	1955 ed.
Gudde, Erwin G. and Elisabeth K., eds.	*From St. Louis to Sutter's Fort, 1846: Journal of Heinrich Lienhard* University of Oklahoma Press, Norman, Okla.	1961 ed.
Hafen & Young	*Fort Laramie 1834–1890* Arthur H. Clark, Glendale, Calif.	1938 ed.
Hammond & Howes, eds.	*Diary of Robert Eccleston* Bancroft-Whitney, San Francisco, Calif.	1950 ed.

Keller, George	*A Trip Across the Plains* Biobooks, Oakland, Calif.	1955 ed.
Lavender, David	*Westward Vision: Oregon Trail* McGraw-Hill, New York, N.Y.	1963 ed.
Meeker, Ezra	*Oregon Trail* Ezra Meeker, New York, N.Y.	1907 ed.
Morgan, Dale	*Overland in 1846,* Vols. I & II Talisman Press, Georgetown, Calif.	1963 ed.
Paden, Irene	*The Wake of the Prairie Schooner* Macmillan, New York, N.Y.	1943 ed.
Parkman, Francis	*The Oregon Trail* New American Library, New York, N.Y.	1964 ed.
Robertson, Frank	*Fort Hall* Hastings House, New York, N.Y.	1963 ed.
Schmitt, Martin F. and Brown, Dee	*The Settler's West* Scribner's, New York, N.Y.	1955 ed.
Spaulding, Kenneth A., ed.	*On the Oregon Trail: Diary of Robert Stuart* University of Oklahoma Press, Norman, Okla.	1953 ed.
Udell, John	*Journal of John Udell* Yale University Press, New Haven, Conn.	1952 ed.
Walker, Henry	*The Wagonmasters* University of Oklahoma Press, Norman, Okla.	1966 ed.

Periodical

| Ridge, Martin | "Why They Went West" *The American West,* Vol. I, No. 3 | 1964 |

Settlement of the Great Plains

Angle, Paul	*The American Reader* Rand McNally, Chicago, Ill.	1958 ed.
Dick, Everett	*The Sod-House Frontier* Johnson, Lincoln, Neb.	1954 ed.
Fite, Gilbert	*The Farmer's Frontier 1865–1900* Holt, Rinehart, Winston, New York, N.Y.	1966 ed.
Kraenzel, Carl	*The Great Plains in Transition* University of Oklahoma Press, Norman, Okla.	1955 ed.
Lamar, Howard	*The Far Southwest 1846–1912* Yale University Press, New Haven, Conn.	1966 ed.

McCullum, H. and F.	*The Wire that Fenced the West* University of Oklahoma Press, Norman, Okla.	1965 ed.
Ruede, Howard	*Sod-House Days 1877–1878* Cooper Square, New York, N.Y.	1966 ed.
Stewart, Elinore	*Letters of a Woman Homesteader* University of Nebraska Press, Lincoln, Neb.	1961 ed.
Webb, Walter	*The Great Plains* Universal Books, New York, N.Y	1931 ed.

Periodicals

| Danker, Donald | "Nebraska Homemade Windmills" *The American West,* Vol. III, No. 1 | 1966 |
| Erdman, Loula | "The Devil's Hatband" *The American West,* Vol. II, No. 1 | 1965 |

General

American Heritage Series	*The Great West* Simon & Schuster, New York, N.Y.	1965 ed.
Billington, Ray Allen	*Westward Expansion* Macmillan, New York, N.Y.	1960 ed.
Clark, Thomas D.	*Frontier America* Scribner's, New York, N.Y.	1959 ed.
Hine, R. V. and Bingham, E. K.	*The Frontier Experience* Wadsworth, Belmont, Calif.	1963 ed.
Richmond and Mardock	*A Nation Moving West* University of Nebraska Press, Lincoln, Neb.	1963 ed.
Smith, Henry Nash	*Virgin Land* Harvard University Press, Cambridge, Mass.	1950 ed.

7 | The Proprietors

How accurate is it to speak of an urban frontier in the United States, particularly as contrasted with a frontier line of settlement? There was indeed a continual wave of town founding and urban development in the West. The variety of forces which stimulated this activity included the discovery of minerals, the cattle industry, the lure of free, fertile land, the effects of war and depression, and certainly the railroad industry.

Perhaps a major oversight in the study of the frontier is the tendency to give the impression that the movement was solely agrarian. While it is true that the farm was the main economic base, the village, the town (particularly the mining town), and in time the city itself, became important elements of the frontier movement. Without Pittsburgh, Cincinnati, Louisville and St. Louis on the earlier frontier, and Chicago, Kansas City, Omaha, Denver and San Francisco on the later one, the West would have lacked the all important centers of supply and distribution.

It was the town and country combined which established a frontier economy and gave a certain cultural tone to the advance of civilization westward. While countrymen struggled with the land, townsmen were struggling to establish hotels, liveries, banks, warehouses, newspapers, schools, theaters, libraries, churches and a functional town government. The frontier town dwellers were pioneers in every sense of the word.

In his discussions of the frontier, Frederick Jackson Turner gave a subordinate role to the city. He implies that the urban frontier is an outgrowth of the four previous frontiers. But another historian, Richard Wade, offers a forceful contrast to Turner.

> The towns were the spearheads of the frontier. Planted far in advance of the line of settlement, they held the West for the approaching population. Indeed, in 1763, when the British threw the Proclamation Line along the Applachians to stop the flow of settlers, a French merchant company prepared to survey the streets of St. Louis, a thousand miles through the wilderness . . . the establishment of towns preceded the breaking of soil in the transmontane west.[1]

Was the urban frontier the first or the last to arrive in the unsettled West? Is city government and the urban frontier class structure in keeping with Turner's assertions on frontier democracy? How reliant was the development of urban centers upon the frontier environment? What role does the city play in bringing culture to the frontier? These questions

[1] Wade, *Urban Frontier,* p. 1.

form the core around which this chapter is built. An historical survey of several western cities, including Kansas City, Santa Fe, Denver, Omaha, Seattle, San Francisco, and a number of others, reveals a highly similar, and in some cases, nearly identical, development. An in-depth study of a single frontier city, rather than the shallow sketches of several, best reveals the importance of the urban frontier.

The city of Denver was selected for this study because its experience in frontier development is most representative of the experiences of urban centers on the frontier, in the late nineteenth century. The most important reason for its selection is the fact that Denver is located at the very center of the region known as the Great West; bounded by the Mississippi River on the east and the Pacific Ocean on the west, Canada on the north and the Rio Grande on the south. In such a location, the "Queen City of the Plains" was continually in touch with the changing tempos of frontier development. It would be very enlightening, however, for each person who reads this chapter to contrast it with a history of his own city.

The Origins of Denver

Occasional probes of the uncharted Rocky Mountain wilderness had been made by some of the frontier's most famous explorers, including Zebulon Pike and John C. Fremont, led by the famous guide, Kit Carson. The accounts of these explorations excited other groups of adventurers to move into the region, first, the mountain men, and then the prospectors. It was from the latter group that the city of Denver emerged.

Numerous trading parties and lone travelers told of rich mineral deposits in the Pikes Peak area. The publication of these stories built up increasing interest in the region, and during the summer of 1858 the first prospecting parties began to arrive. The William Green Russell party came all

the way from Georgia, made a placer strike near present-day
Englewood, Colorado, and after exhausting it, moved north.
The news trickled into Kansas and from Lawrence came the
group which established the first permanent settlement. On
September 6, 1858, they organized the Montana Town
Company and assigned a civil engineer to survey and lay out
Montana City. A dispute over the location resulted in part
of the Lawrence party breaking away, moving farther north,
and on September 24, organizing the St. Charles Town As-
sociation.

Considerable attention was given to the selection of a
proper site for the latter settlement. The experience of town
proprietorship had taught these men to locate on a major
traffic artery. St. Charles was consequently established near
the Platte River-Cherry Creek junction, which was also the
intersection of a trapper's trace and military trail from Fort
Bridger to New Mexico.

Late in October the Russell party returned from the north
and decided to found a settlement of their own on the south
side of Cherry Creek, opposite St. Charles. On November 1,
the constitution for the Auraria Town Company was for-
mally adopted.

Two weeks later a Kansas prospecting party under the
leadership of General William Larimer, an experienced
banker, railroad builder, politician and city founder, arrived at the rivers' junction. The Larimer group immediately
jumped the St. Charles land claim and on November 22,
established the Denver City Company. They proceeded to
form a claim club to preserve their claims.

Conceived in claim-jumping and coercive tactics, it was
inevitable that trouble should emerge between the neighboring settlements of Auraria and Denver. Even during times
of hardship, the promoters of the two communities advertised their civic pride to the point of appearing ridiculous.
Bitter rivalry resulted and the two settlements contested each
other's claims to population supremacy, the first white birth,
the first bank, the first school and the first anything that

seemed to be what a proper town ought to have. The rivalry
was reflected in a letter written in the spring of 1859 by an
overzealous resident of Denver City.

Them Southern desperadoes from Georgia that
located their city on the west side of Cherry Creek
have reached the end of their rope. They have lied
about our townsite . . . . wherever they had a
chance to wag a tongue or write a letter. But their
doom is sealed already and Denver is the city of
the present and the future. We have thirty-eight
beautiful and substantial building in our town
now, while them contumacious villains has but
eighty. Theirs are huts and hovels and shanties
that you wouldn't drive a cow into for shelter,
while ours are to be called palaces by comparison.
We have named our city after Gov. Denver, as
fine a gentleman as ever set foot on the soil of
Kansas, while them braggarts have gone to the
poetry book for a name—and they'll go to the devil
for a history . . . . They think because they have
got the newspaper and the express office that
Denver City is done for. If you hear any of their
lies back in the States, contradict them . . . . They
are making a great hullabaloo because they have
got the first board roof . . . a good mud roof ain't a
thing to be despised in a dry country like this. If
they are well made, there is no particular danger of
them washing down on a family . . . . 'Tisn't as
if pioneers were sporting velvet carpets and satin
upholstery that a little stream of muddy water
running down here and there would spoil . . . . No,
sir, friend Witter, Denver City is the bobtail hoss
that I have bet all my money on and you and me
will live to see marble palaces lining its streets
. . . . Now Larimer and me and the rest of us fellows want you to come out this summer and put
your shoulders to the wheel with us and you'll
make a fortune . . . . The plains are covered with
posies now and the mountains are a sight you will

> never see anywhere else out of Paradise. Every-
> body is well—nobody gets sick here, not even over
> in Auraria, where you'd think people would want
> to die just to get away from it.[2]

Occasionally the rivalry erupted into violence, and in every dispute the first question asked was, "Are you a Denver man or an Aurarian?" The community feud was finally solved when Golden City, some ten miles west of Denver, indicated ambitions of becoming territorial capital, creating a need for consolidation of the two Cherry Creek settlements. Neither settlement was much by itself, but by putting the two together they could create a presentable town to serve as the capital. The unification was officially completed when the territorial legislature granted a charter and a joint election was held for mayor in December of 1859. Denver dates from these beginnings but, according to the historian Robert Perkins, through an illegal act by the legislature with no authority and an election of dubious validity.

At the time of unification the settlement consisted of cabins roughly built out of materials which were readily available to a man more interested in panning for gold than building a house. These materials were normally cotton-wood logs, mud and prairie sod.

The people who composed the early settlement came from all walks of life, driven by many reasons. Many had been bankrupt by the 1857 depression; others had broken laws in the East, but generally they came for fame and fortune. Consequently, historians record opposing views of the type and quality of population which founded early Denver. The very enthusiastic Jerome Smiley writes in *The History of Denver*:

> To assert or imply that as a whole the mass was
> composed of bankrupts, criminals, gamblers, and
> loafers, is stupid, ignorant nonsense, formulated

[2] Mumey, *History of the Early Settlement of Denver,* pp. 190–94.

from the stories it was once common to relate of
many places in the west . . . as to loafers, this
country was probably the most uninviting region
in the world for them. The truth is that while
many had been bankrupted, and many others im-
poverished by the collapse in 1857, in the main
the men who came here in the pioneer times were
of average honesty, and of more than average enthusiasm and heedlessness. They were inspired by
no worse motive than one to better their worldly
condition . . . .

The majority of Denver historians, including contemporaries of the period, present a description of lawlessness,
thievery, murder on a daily schedule, rampant prostitution
and universal gambling. One eyewitness to the extent of the
community's gambling habits allegedly saw the probate
judge of the county lose thirty Denver lots in less than ten
minutes in a public saloon on Sunday morning. Shortly
afterward he observed the county sheriff pawning his revolver for twenty dollars to spend in betting at faro.

The historian, Stanley Zamonski, records that one-tenth
of the population lived on the profits of prostitution. Perkins
quotes a contemporary citizen as stating that the other nine-
tenths of the population lived on the profits of gambling. If
these accounts are assumed to be only partially accurate,
they would cast some suspicion on Smiley's complimentary
description.

The origins of the city of Denver were not unlike those
which typified many western towns, fated to boom fantasti-
cally, only to disappear into oblivion. Denver City successfully avoided that fate because of the quality and experience
of her early leadership. The men who founded the community
were experienced city founders. They selected the most favorable location, organized formal town companies and even had
a civil engineer survey and stake out their settlement. The
object of these leaders was to found a city rather than spec-

ulate in the gold-fields and consequently, they made their profits selling plots of land through the town company. Their optimism and their knowledge of what causes a city to succeed or fail is reflected in a speech delivered by William Larimer during the winter of 1858 following the creation of the Denver City Company.

> We are satisfied with our prospects here and intend to stay until this country is fully explored. . . . The late financial panic which has prostrated every branch of trade will bring an influx of enterprising people . . . . A railroad is coming. The Pacific Railroad has planned to build through the West. And even without a branch at this point we can tap it at the crossing of the North and South Platte . . . . The whole country is demanding that this road be built. The West is demanding it. Denver City demands it . . . . Manifest Destiny has shaped its end. We have laid the foundation for a city, an outlet for this gold bonanza and for the Rocky Mountain Region.[3]

Historian Stanley Zamonski suggests that the migrations which halted at the Platte-Cherry Creek Rivers junction proceeded to build a town to feed, clothe and shelter them and provide whiskey, cards, and women.

The Economic Base of Denver

The Denver City Company used devious methods to lure settlers into the region. They spread and published false reports about rich gold discoveries in the Rocky Mountain area. Later when large numbers of people who had been unsuccessful in their prospecting began returning to the East,

[3] Zamonski & Keller, *The Fifty-Niners,* p. 18. (Sage Books) The Swallow Press, Inc., Chicago, Ill.

the company was faced with disaster. The opportune visit of Horace Greeley, in June, 1859, assisted in halting the eastward movement. Greeley announced to his Eastern readers:

> I have seen with my own eyes and have been convinced by the work of my hands. Go west, young man, go west! [4]

The gold rush of 1859 followed shortly afterwards.

Denver City became the focal point of the redistribution of people and the exchange of goods. With the influx of prospectors during the spring of 1859, the population of Denver soared and by March the inhabitants numbered 600.

Business houses were set up one after the other to handle the needs of the growing population for consumer goods. To service these businesses and the expanding population, banking was provided. The first business established in the Cherry Creek community was the Blake-Williams general merchandise house. It was soon followed by a hardware store and by December of 1858, there was a jewelry store, blacksmith shop and carpenter shop. Christmas day was celebrated with the opening of the settlement's first saloon. Shortly after the first of the year, the Eldorado Hotel opened along with the town's first bakery and drugstore. By July, 1860, the city had its first bank and mint. Consequently, Denver became an important center of capital.

The problem of feeding, clothing, arming and equipping the new emigrants put a strain on the already over-taxed transportation facilities. There were no railroads west of the Missouri River and everything had to be freighted in by wagon. On May 7, 1859, the first stagecoach arrived in Denver and ten days later the first Leavenworth to Pikes Peak express coach completed its nineteen-day trip across the Plains.

The major objective of Denver City's leadership through-

[4] *Ibid.,* p. 36.

out the 1860's was to secure a position on the route of the transcontinental railroad. In November, 1866, the Union Pacific announced its decision to build across the plains of Wyoming, instead of through Denver. The city was stunned, but some of the more aggressive citizens, led by John Evans, raised enough money to finance the Denver-Pacific Railroad, which tapped the main line in Cheyenne on June 22, 1870. In the first month the railroad carried over one thousand passengers to Denver and thirteen million pounds of freight. Denver began to grow as never before. The population in 1870 was 4,759 and ten years later it numbered 35,629.

The year of 1870 stands as a line of demarcation in the economic history of Denver, but it is not all due to the arrival of railroads. Placer mining had passed its peak in 1860. The gold seekers turned to tunnel and drift mining which required a large investment and was considerably slower. Assays proved the gold was there but the limited metallurgical knowledge and refining methods failed to recover it. Then, in January of 1868, the first smelter was fired in Black Hawk, Colorado. Deep rock mining, long the nemesis of prospectors, suddenly began to pay dividends to mining companies. This was the major reason railroads began to expand their operations, because Denver became the supply point for all the activity in the mountain towns. From 1858 to 1870, Colorado mines produced thirty-three million dollars in gold. The output climbed steadily thereafter, reaching a high of $235,000,000 in the first decade of the twentieth century.

In addition to gold mining the first major silver discovery was made in 1864. For thirty years, silver was more lucrative than gold and more than any single factor brought wealth to Denver.

The city became largely self-sustaining. Very few succeeded at agriculture, but those who did became exceptionally wealthy. Cattle raising flourished on the prairies and in the mountains until the middle 1880's. Denver served as the market for both cattle and sheep, and became the big cow town of the region, developing stockyards and packing houses.

A variety of things composed the economic base of Denver, and each had its turn emerging as the dominant economic force. An accurate economic description of Denver during its first decade would be to say that it was the marketing distributing and coinage center of the Pikes Peak region.

Emergence of Urban Problems

One of the most pressing urban problems in Denver City was its high rate of crime. It had developed a coast-to-coast reputation as a wide open town. Part of the problem can be attributed to the unusually rapid increase in population which usually brought with it a decline in moral standards.

Saloons, among the first established business houses in the community, were the source of much of the lawlessness. Because few evenings passed in these saloons without a gun fight, the musicians in these gambling houses lined the low enclosures surrounding the bandstand with sheet iron. The historian Stanley Zamonski reports that a good orchestra, at the first shot, could vanish behind the armored enclosure, then come up into the gunsmoke playing without losing a beat.

Most of the inhabitants relied on their weapons to arbitrate their disputes. The first fifteen people buried in the town cemetery died of gunshot wounds. If a fair fight resulted in death, no questions were asked. If the killing was obviously murder, the victim's friends usually apprehended the killer and hanged him.

The general character of law and order is described in a letter written October 4, 1859, in Denver City by Libeus Barney.

Some time since, a barber, and a butcher got into a quarrel in Auraria, the latter knocking the former down, and on his recovery, the knight of the razor drew a knife, and with desperation inflicted five separate wounds in the abdomen of his antagonist. The barber was arrested, tried for murder, but the remarkable evidence that usually attends the defense in similar cases, was not wanting in this, and the *justifiable homicide* now parades the streets free as the winds . . . . At Golden City, last month, a gambler, while on a spree, was flourishing his bowie knife and revolver, threatening to take the life of anyone who should have the presumption to obstruct his pathway. He had his career suddenly brought to a close by an infuriated mob, who seized, bound, tied and hung the desperado all within the short time of twenty minutes; believing the adage that "an ounce of preventative is worth a pound of cure." There is scarcely a day revolves, but some one crime or another is committed; theft, robbery or murder.[5]

Law and order finally arrived in May of 1861 with territorial Governor William Gilpin. He had a system of courts functioning by July 10; and in September, the legislature enacted a civil and criminal code, establishing penalties for counterfeiting gold dust and coins.

Due to the widespread use of wooden construction, Denver was extremely vulnerable to fire. In addition to the extensive use of lumber, the inhabitants were careless in other ways with fire. They had casually burned off forests around mountain diggings, left their campfires smoldering for days, set prairie fires, and stored gunpowder in shacks. It was not until July 15, 1862, that the city council decided to correct the total absence of fire-fighting facilities. Along with a volunteer hook and ladder company, bucket brigades were also organized. However, the cart and buckets were still on

[5] Barney, *Letters of the Pikes Peak Gold Rush,* pp. 47–8.

order and the fire department only on paper when the $350,000 fire of April 19, 1863 occurred. The "Great Fire of '63" became the dividing line between architectural eras. Denver re-built largely with brick and began to take on an urban appearance. Fire hydrants were finally installed in April of 1871.

Flooding was also a problem which revealed carelessness on the part of the town builders. Many of the business houses built so close to the rivers that they were forced to put down pilings to get a firm foundation. On three occasions, 1864, 1878, and 1885, Cherry Creek flooded and washed out everything close to its banks.

A problem which all towns had in common was the care of streets. Denver was not an exception. The planners did have the foresight to construct the streets eighty feet wide which allowed for greater safety. They did not make any provision for paving, however, and consequently, the streets were either muddy or dusty. Pedestrians had to be especially alert for galloping horses, rubbish and criminals. The problem was compounded at night, due to the absence of street lights, which were not installed until the coming of gas lights in 1871. Wandering livestock was an additional street hazard. As late as 1880, marksmen were still shooting wild antelope on the main street of the community.

Still another problem was the supply of water. The first residents of Denver drank directly from the rivers. Later, well water was sold by the bottle or bucket, which became a big business even after the citizens began to dig their own wells. Surface wells and bottles of water were not sufficient for a town the size of Denver. In January, 1872, the Denver City Water Company piped the first water into Denver homes from the underground flow of Cherry Creek. Later in 1872, Denver homes began to get indoor plumbing.

The development of technology in Denver followed the same pace as most everything else, reaching a peak in the 1870's. The telegraph had arrived in 1863, but the telephone didn't come until 1879.

Although the town government of Denver was badly organized in the beginning, it was better developed than any other territorial or state organization. The city elections were often very questionable. Sometimes they were 200 or 300 votes in an area consisting of twelve eligible voters. Finally, in October of 1859, after Denver received its official charter and elected its first mayor, the community was more successfully governed by a town council.

As pointed out earlier in this chapter, there was a strong rivalry betwen Auraria and Denver City. Even after the merger, the Civil War nearly divided the communities again. This community competition had its harmful effects on the development of Denver, but one might also suggest that it prodded the settlement to develop more quickly than would have been the case if either town had been isolated.

Finally, the settlement had to deal at irregular intervals with an Indian problem. The relationship between Denver and the various tribes of Indians in Colorado was neither cordial, nor critical. The Indians antagonized the settlers by doing such things as severing the telegraph wires and on one occasion, preventing the supply trains from reaching Denver. They occasionally outraged the Denver citizens by commiting a massacre, but the Denverites retaliated at Sand Creek in November of 1864. All in all, the Indian problem was never a serious one.

The emergence of these urban problems forced a civic responsibility upon the community, which it finally assumed in full measure during the second decade of its history.

Social Structure and Activities of Denver

Culture and learning followed the prospectors to the Denver City settlement within a year. In the early fall of 1859, the settlement's first book store was opened. By November a circulating library was in operation. In the cultural history of Denver City the date of October 3, 1859, is auspicious.

Early that day, Professor O. J. Goldrick opened the settlement's first school. That same evening saw the town's first theatrical opening night. Colonel Thorne's theatrical troupe came south from Laramie, Wyoming, and opened *The Maid in Croissey* in Apollo Hall. The opening was described in a letter written the following day.

> Last night was ushered in an event of paramount interest to Pike's Peakers. Mr. Charles Thom, the far-famed itinerant theatrical showman, with a company of eleven performers, made their debut at "Apollo Hall", before a large, though not very remarkable select audience. Admittance, one dollar; comfortable accommodations for three hundred and fifty; receipts, 400, which tells well for the patronage, if not for the appreciation of are in this semi-barbarous region.[6]

Within a week, frontier show business prompted competition from the neighboring settlement of Auraria. Cibola Hall was rebuilt and a large number of would-be thespians hired from the gold fields. Insulted, Colonel Thorne left Denver, but the theater was there to stay. It thrived during the following years with the opening of the Denver Theater in November, 1860, and finally reached a peak with the construction of the Tabor Grand Opera House in the 1880's. The life and legend of the Tabor family was recently made the subject of the popular opera, *The Ballad of Baby Doe*.

The Union School founded by O. J. Goldrick was the forerunner of the first public schools of 1862, though it was not until 1872 that Denver built its first school house. Attention was also given to higher education in Denver. Early in 1863, proposals were announced for a seminary, and on September 10, the *Rocky Mountain News* carried the following news item.

[6] Barney, *op. cit.*, p. 50.

> The University building is being pushed forward rapidly and when finished will compare most favorably with any similar structure west of St. Louis.

The building was completed by Christmas and the school opened in 1864. By 1880 it became known as the University of Denver.

Probably the greatest stimulant to Denver culture was the arrival of the railroad in 1870. Along with thousands of immigrants, it brought a number of celebrities to the region who left marked effects on the thinking Denverites. In addition to celebrities the railroad brought new styles, ideas, and trends which slowly began to alter some of the provincial aspects of Denver society.

At the very heart of nearly every element in Denver's early history was the *Rocky Mountain News*. The paper survived the fire of '63, the flood of '64 and countless competitors, and through it all supported almost every civic achievement Denver attained. It advertised the gold strikes, advocated territorial status and later statehood, supported the railroad connection with Cheyenne, aided the development of higher education, and pushed for a whole series of urban improvements. From 1867 to 1876, thirty-two newspapers were founded in Denver, but all of them eventually failed and only the *News* remained. The *Rocky Mountain News* was the single most important unifying element in the settlement and it grew in proportion with the town.

Class structure and social snobbery in Denver date back to the construction of the settlement's first cabin. Denver's first cabin was erected on a site which was regarded as an early slum. The early historians were conscious of social distinction and made it plain that a hut built by a low trapper could not qualify in their annals of civic progress. An alternate cabin was therefore selected.

During the early years the social structure was not very

rigidly defined. It wasn't until the middle 1870's and the 1880's that the city became socially stratified; and as they looked back to the early years, they attempted to stratify their origins as well. During this later period the silver kings began to build their elaborate mansions. Society editors were always interested in the activities of "The Sacred Thirty-Six," led by Mrs. Crawford Hill. Many of the wives, including Baby Doe Tabor, Mrs. J. J. "Molly" Brown and the Baroness Louise von Richthofen discovered that they were socially unacceptable to "The Sacred Thirty-Six." Influenced by these ladies, some of the men had to re-organize their clubs to drop undesirables.

Racial tolerance did not extend itself to the so-called Yellow Peril. By 1880 there were 238 Chinese in Denver, laborers who remained after the completion of the transcontinental railroad. They lived in a section referred to as "Chink Alley," and were the brunt of the city's "Chink, Chink Chinaman" songs. A political slogan in 1880 read, "The Chinese must go."

The first Negroes arrived with the Russell party from Georgia in 1858. In the early years of the Denver City settlement, restrictions were placed on Negroes by the territorial by-laws of 1861–1865. They were not allowed to serve on juries or attend schools, but they were allowed to vote and they also paid taxes. By 1865, a Negro school was established in Denver, and Coles Hall became the social center of all Negro activities. In 1868, a Negro Mason's lodge was organized. A few of the Negroes such as Jim Beckwourth, were quite wealthy, but the majority were not.

Denver's first church, lodge and Ladies' Aid Society were all functioning by late 1859. Their influence was usually overshadowed by the influence of Denver's saloons.

Again the year 1870 emerges as the line of division in Denver's social history. The rise of the railroad builders and silver kings had a tendency to create rigid cleavages in Denver's social structure, produce racial intolerance and bring a greater appreciation to cultural and philanthropic activities.

Comparison and Conclusion

Because the pattern of organization for this chapter is based upon Carl Bridenbaugh's *Cities in the Wilderness* and Richard Wade's *The Urban Frontier,* it seemed that it would be helpful to make a brief comparison of the growth of Denver with city growth on these previous frontiers.

The cities described by Bridenbaugh were founded in approximately 1630. They were under the control of, governed by and, in many cases, founded by the Church. Those highest on the social ladder were the clergy. This stands in contrast to the cities described by Wade—particularly Denver. The Church was probably the most ineffective institution in early Denver as contrasted with the Boston of Cotton and Increase Mather. The cities presented in Wade's book were controlled, governed and founded by a group of wealthy individuals. This also holds true for the founding and governing of Denver.

	Population		
Bridenbaugh: 1630		Wade: 1770	Denver: 1858
10 yrs. 400		400	4,500
20 yrs. 1000		750	35,000
30 yrs. 2000		1200	105,000

The population growth in both groups of early cities was much more gradual than Denver experienced. Consequently, urban problems were not forced upon them as quickly as they were upon Denver. Even though the saloon was a major social institution in all of these cities, the difficulty it presented seemed to be magnified in Denver. The problem

217

of crime and lawlessness in all of these cities grew in proportion to the population.

Fifty years elapsed before the first coastal city acquired fire-fighting equipment and began building with brick. The same process required approximately twenty-five years in the Ohio Valley cities, but only five years in Denver.

The first newspapers did not appear in Bridenbaugh's cities for seventy-five years. Wade's cities acquired them within fifteen years, and the *Rocky Mountain News* was published in Denver six months after the first settlement arrived.

In the first urban developments, it required sixty years before they began naming and lighting its twenty-four foot wide streets. Within thirteen years Denver had accomplished this civic responsibility on its eighty foot streets.

To both the coastal and Ohio Valley cities the Negro minority constituted one of their most formidable difficulties. It was never a severe problem in Denver. The sailors in the first group of cities and the rivermen and wagonmen in the second group of cities occupied the same social position that the lowly trappers held in Denver.

Perhaps the differentiation of time in the development of the cities can be accounted for by looking at the much improved system of transportation and communication, which in Denver's day could transport people and ideas from coast to coast in a comparatively short period of time. Consequently population could increase at an enormous rate and the urban problems and civic achievements would increase at the same rate.

The discussion thus far has centered upon the contrasts of city development in the three eras. There were similarities which should be mentioned as well. Spanning the two-hundred-year period was the problem of the American Indian. Every city mentioned faced this situation and had to create its own solution to the problem. In addition, all of these cities had in common the problem of good transportation connections. The ocean was to the coastal cities what the river and steamboat were to the Ohio Valley cities and in turn what the railroad was to Denver. The fear of failure and the struggle for survival and then supremacy was common to them all and resulted in a competitive relationship with neighboring settlements.

Denver, unlike many other residential settlements, was founded with the stated intention of creating a city and was fortunate to have had experienced and civic-minded founders.

> They had given birth, at the foot of the Rockies, to a lusty, squawling, infant city. The howling baby had teethed on a six-shooter and nursed on a whiskey bottle, and had learned to crawl over floods and under flying bullets . . . . Already the child could stand on wobbly legs.[7]

Bibliography

General Urban Histories

Bridenbaugh, Carl	*Cities in the Wilderness* Alfred A. Knopf, New York, N.Y.	1938 ed.
Glaab, Charles	*The American City: A Documentary History* Dorsey Press, Homewood, Ill.	1963 ed.
Green, Constance	*American Cities in the Growth of the Nation* Harper (Colophon Books), New York, N.Y.	1957 ed.
McKelvey, Blake	*The Urbanization of America, 1860 to 1915* Rutgers University Press, New Brunswick, N.J.	1963 ed.
Mumford, Lewis	*The City in History* Harcourt, Brace & World, New York, N.Y.	1961 ed.
Schlesinger, Arthur	*The Rise of the City, 1878–1898* Macmillan, New York, N.Y.	1933 ed.
Wade, Richard	*The Urban Frontier* Harvard University Press, Boston, Mass.	1959 ed.

[7] Zamonski, *op. cit.*, pp. 269–70.

Denver Histories

Anderson, George	*Colorado Railroad Building, 1870–1880* Colorado College, Colorado Springs, Colo.	1936 ed.
Bancroft, Caroline	*Mile High Denver* Golden Press, Lakewood, Colo.	1952 ed.
Barney, Libeus	*Letters of the Pikes Peak Gold Rush* Talisman Press, San Jose, Calif.	1959 ed.
Fowler, Gene	*Timber Line* Covici-Fried, New York, N.Y.	1933 ed.
Kohl, Edith	*Denver's Historic Mansions* (Sage Books) The Swallow Press, Inc., Chicago, Ill.	1957 ed.
Mumey, Nolie	*Clark, Gruber and Company: A Pioneer Denver Mint* Artcraft Press, Denver, Colo.	1950 ed.
Mumey, Nolie	*History of Early Denver* Arthur H. Clark, Glendale, Calif.	1942 ed.
Parkhill, Forbes	*Wildest of the West* Sage Books, Denver, Colo.	1957 ed.
Perkin, Robert	*The First Hundred Years* Doubleday, Garden City, N.Y.	1959 ed.
Smiley, Jerome	*History of Denver* Times and Sun Publishing Company, Denver, Colo.	1901 ed.
Vickers, William	*History of Denver* Buskin, Chicago, Ill.	1880 ed.
Wharton, Junius	*History of the City of Denver* Byers, Denver, Colo.	1866 ed.
Zamonski, Stanley	*The Fifty-niners* (Sage Books) The Swallow Press, Inc., Chicago, Ill.	1961 ed.

8 | The Frontier and the American Character

There is far from complete agreement as to what is or is not uniquely American. In the case of practically every trait which an author alleges to be characteristically American, there is a contradictory trait which another author also believes to be distinctively American. The people of America are described as generous and niggardly, sympathetic and unfeeling, idealistic and cynical, visionary and practical—hence, an endless list which cancels itself out. Emerging from a thorough study of American character traits is the distinct revelation that diversity is perhaps the most fundamental trait of all. With the great variety of races and cultures which have been forged into a single American nationality, it is not surprising that the end result bears strong resemblance to a mosaic.

Authorities suggest that the combined impact of a wide variety of historical forces created a unique national character for Americans. These forces are no less diverse or contradictory than the traits they produced. Material abundance, mobility, technology and industrialism, a European heritage, a frontier environment—all of these and more have been supported as major forces in character styling.

> One can go into a wild country and make it tame, but, like a coat and cap and mittens that he can never take off, he must always carry the look of land as it was. He can drive the plough . . . make fields and roads go every way, build him a fine house and wear the stiff collar, and yet he will always look like the grass where the buffalo have eaten and smell of the new ground his feet have walked on.[1]

Many authorities in addition to Frederick Jackson Turner have proposed that the American environment had a very formidable influence upon the fabric of a distinctive American character. The substance of this argument was established in the first appraisal of the American character ever to be designed.

"What then is the American, this new man?" The study of American character began with this question posed by the French immigrant, Crevecoeur, in the late eighteenth century. A bold writer of romantic style, he penned the following description of an American:

> *He* is an American, who leaving behind him all his ancient prejudices and manners, receives new ones from the new mode of life he has embraced, the new government he obeys, and the new rank he

[1] From *Old Jules* (Flyleaf) by Mari Sandoz. (By permission of University of Nebraska Press, © 1966.)

> holds . . . . Here individuals of all nations are
> melted into a new race of men . . . . The American
> is a new man, who acts upon new principles; he
> must therefore entertain new ideas, and form new
> opinions. From involuntary idleness, servile de-
> pendence, penury, and useless labour, he has
> passed to toils of a very different nature, rewarded
> by ample subsistence—This is an American.[2]

Crevecoeur produced this pioneer examination of the
American character at a time when political union was only
recently contrived and the former British subjects were far
from possessing a sense of common nationality. It was very
doubtful that a durable nation, much less a national character, could be created out of thirteen ill-sorted states.

What possible similarities could be found among persons
so diverse as a Nantucket fisherman, a Broad Street lawyer in
Philadelphia, an aristocratic planter of the Chesapeake, a
Bay Street merchant in Charlestown, a crude backwoodsman
of the Ohio valley, and a frugal Yankee farmer? Crevecoeur
was alert to the broad heterogeneity of the people.

> Exclusive of those general characteristics, each
> province has its own, founded on the government,
> climate, mode of husbandry, customs and peculi-
> arity of circumstances. Europeans . . . became in
> the course of a few generations, not only Ameri-
> cans in general, but either Pennsylvanians, Virgin-
> ians, or provincials under some other name. Who-
> ever traverses the continent must easily observe
> those strong differences, which will grow more
> evident in time.[3]

Yet behind all the distinctions he detected a common type,
fashioned from a common experience; and in order to ex-

[2] From *Letters From an American Farmer* by J. Hector St. John de
Crevecoeur, London, 1782.
[3] *Ibid.*

plain the "common experience," Crevecoeur relied heavily upon the force of "environment." Crevecoeur asserted that immigrants to America were transformed into "a new race of men" by the action upon them of the natural and cultural environment.

> Everything has tended to regenerate them; new laws, a new mode of living, a new social system; here they are become men: In Europe they were as so many useless plants, wanting vegetative mould, and refreshing showers; they withered, and were mowed down by want, hunger, and war; but now by the power of transplantation, like all other plants they have taken root and flourished . . . . Men are like plants; the goodness and flavour of the fruit proceeds from the peculiar soil and exposition in which they grow. We are nothing but what we derive from the air we breathe, the climate we inhabit, the government we obey, the system of religion we profess, and the nature of our employment . . . .[4]

Crevecoeur's observations, particularly his portrait of the American farmer as the model of the dominant traits of the American character, closely resemble the very heart of the Turner Thesis. As revealed in Chapter One of this book, Frederick Jackson Turner obviously regarded the frontier experience as the pre-eminent factor in the formation of the national character. His interpretation, also governed by the principle of environment, named the pioneer as the archetypical American. Turner suggested that the distinctively national features of the American character were sculptured by the people's triumphant encounter with the western wilderness. His writing is very much in harmony with the observations of Crevecoeur, recorded more than 100 years before.

> He who would wish to see America in its proper light, and have a true idea of its feeble beginnings

[4] *Ibid.*

and barbarous rudiments, must visit our extended
line of frontiers where the last settlers dwell, and
where he 'may see the first labours of settlement,
the mode of clearing the earth . . . . They are a
kind of forlorn hope, preceding by ten or twelve
years the most respectable army of veterans which
come after them. In that space, prosperity will
polish some, vice and the law will drive off the
rest, who uniting again with others like themselves
will recede still farther; making room for more
industrious people, who will finish their improvements, convert the loghouse into a convenient
habitation, and rejoicing that the first heavy labours are finished, will change in a few years that
hitherto barbarous country into a fine fertile, well
regulated district. Such is our progress, such is the
march of the Europeans toward the interior parts
of this continent.[5]

Was Turner or Crevecoeur the author of the preceding
quotation? Contrary to what you may have guessed, the
answer is Crevecoeur, and it should serve to point out the
very close similarity in the thoughts of the two men.

Crevecoeur recorded his observations toward the end of
the eighteenth century while Turner did not give birth to his
views until the close of the nineteenth century. By the mid-
twentieth century numerous historians, including Arthur
Schlesinger, Ray Allen Billington, Everett Dick, Walter
Webb and others, *continued* to emphasize the influence of a
frontier environment upon the fabric of American culture.
Although insisting that due attention be given to "Old
World Influence," Arthur Schlesinger eloquently described
the force of environment in an article prepared for the
American Historical Review in 1943.

It has often been observed that plants and animals
undergo modification when removed to America.

[5] *Ibid.*

225

These mutations arise from differences in climate and geography. But other factors as well affected transplanted people. One was the temperament of the settler, the fact that he was more adventurous, more ambitious or more rebellious against conditions at home than his fellows. It is not necessary to believe with William Stoughton in 1670 that "God sifted a whole Nation that he might send Choice Grain over into this Wilderness," but undoubtedly the act of quitting a familiar existence for a strange and perilous one demanded uncommon attributes of hardihood, self-reliance and imagination. Once the ocean was crossed, sheer distance from the old country and the challenge of new experiences further weakened the bonds of custom, evoked latent capacities and awakened the settler to possibilities of improvement hitherto unsuspected. The *undeveloped continent prescribed the conditions of living the new life, the mold within which the American character took shape* . . . . Based upon the solid qualities of those Europeans who planted the colonies, it (national character) assumed distinctive form under pressure of adaptation to the radically different situation. "Our ancestors sought a new continent," said James Russell Lowell. "What they found was a new condition of mind." The protracted tutelage to the soil acted as the chief formative influence, dispelling ancient inhibitions, freeing dormant energies, revamping mental attitudes.[6]

One of America's most distinguished frontier historians was the late Walter Prescott Webb. He wrote that it would require a strongly perverse mind to deny that the long process of moving and occupying raw land left any effects. Professor Webb developed the idea of a frontier environment much

[6] Schlesinger, Arthur, *Paths to the Present,* Macmillan, 1949, p. et passim.

further than most authors. He lifted the Turner Thesis out of its narrow American encasement and applied it to the whole world. The idea of a world frontier, which Webb explored in one of his most provocative books, *The Great Frontier,* has become known as the Webb Thesis. Discussing the time period from 1500 to 1900, Webb called attention to the many frontier settlements founded by European nations as they expanded into the continents of Africa and Australia as well as North and South America. He described Western Europe as the East in the American sense, bearing the same relation to the great frontier that the Atlantic coast settlements long bore to the traditional American West. Webb identified Western Europe as the "metropolis," thus setting it apart from the great frontier, and then proceeded to describe the impact of the two forces interacting.

> When . . . we observe the interaction between the Metropolis and the Great Frontier over a period of four and one-half centuries, we feel that we have perhaps found one of the important keys to modern Western civilization . . . . This interaction between these two gigantic forces developed so much power that, like a diesel engine, it picked up all the other historical movements, such as the price revolution, the commercial revolution, the industrial revolution, and the democratic revolutions, and moved them like a long train down the track. Whatever got in the way of this interaction was altered or destroyed; whatever harmonized with it or served it, prospered. In the long perspective, both capitalism and democracy appear as by-products of the interaction, the use of the precious metals as a medium of exchange appears as an episode now ended, and the rise of modern Negro slavery appears as a device adopted by the Metropolitans in order that they might have cheap and permanent labor with which to hew their fortunes out of the raw materials of the Great

Frontier. Before this interaction, the old ideas about economics, based on scarcity, were wrecked because they were not applicable to the new age of plenty. Mercantilism gave way to laissez faire, which lasted only as long as the frontier lasted. These are some of the vistas that open up when we view the whole Frontier and its relation to the whole Metropolis, vistas which cannot ordinarily be reached by the most minute examination of a single frontier fragment.[7]

Walter Webb felt very deeply about his subject and lamented the conditions produced by what he identified as the "death" of the great frontier.

By 1900 or thereabout, the first phase was over because the Metropolis had in effect eaten up the Frontier . . . . There is no longer the dramatic interaction to which I have attributed such power and influence. There is no longer the dynamism to which we were accustomed, no longer the free migration of people or the return cargoes of windfall wealth. Many practices, ideas, and institutions which arose and served well when the interaction was going on have been discarded, and all—even democracy and capitalism—are being modified . . . . What we view now is a condition created by the cessation of the interaction. There is no interaction because one of the leading characters is dead. The Metropolis has destroyed the Frontier and stands triumphant in the midst of the magnificent ruins.[8]

[7] Reprinted with permission of the copyright owners, The Regents of the University of Wisconsin, from Walker D. Wyman & Clifton B. Kroeber, eds., *The Frontier in Perspective*, pp. 115–7, 1957, The University of Wisconsin Press.
[8] Webb, *op. cit.*

Conflicting Views

Other authorities, pursuing their investigations into the American character, offer evidence to support alternative forces to that of environment. They do not deny the importance of a frontier environment but instead point to its limitations and suggest that it should only be considered in conjunction with other forces.

It should be noted that a comparison of the effects of frontier movements in North America, South America, Russia, Africa, and Australia reveals a significant diversity. The traits of democracy, freedom and individualism—so long identified as attributes of the American frontier environment —rarely appear among those traits resulting from the frontier movements in much of Latin America, Africa and Russia.

A comparison of national characters on the five major continents points up more contrasts than similarities. The important fact emerges that even though there were frontier conditions and movements on all of these continents, each national character is distinctive. One might easily conclude that other forces as well as a frontier environment play an important role in the styling of a national character.

If the frontier did not produce the traits ascribed to it, what did? The historian, Carlton Hayes, concluded that the American character was due in large part to the force of "European Heritage" which gradually overpowered the frontier environment.

Other authorities developed still newer theories on the design of American character. Turner, himself, had stressed the *movement* of Americans across the face of the continent. Later writers developed the idea of movement into a full-blown theory of social mobility, in which the taming of a frontier environment occupied a restricted role. George W. Pierson, a professor at Yale University, is one of the most articulate spokesmen of this theory which he identifies as the "M-Factor" in American history.

> What made and kept us different was not just the wilderness of the North American continent, nor its vast empty spaces, nor even its wealth of resources, powerful as must have been those influences. No. It was, first of all, the M-Factor: the factor of movement, migration, mobility. Colonization was one part of it; immigration, another; the westward movement itself was a fraction, but only a fraction, of the whole. This whole began with many old-world uprootings. It gathered force with the transatlantic passage. It flooded on to the farmlands of the mid-continent. But increasingly it meant movement also *away* from the frontier, from farm to town, from region to region, from city to city. Individuals, families, churches, villages, on occasion whole countrysides, have participated—and continue to participate.[9]

Among other things, Turner had also defined the frontier as the abundance of free land. By the 1950's historians were exploring the implications of abundance in general for the development of the national character. In his book, *The American Experience* (p. 8), the historian Henry Parkes commented:

> ... unexampled abundance of land and resources was the cardinal factor in the development of American civilization. It molded the character of the American people, and was the chief reason for the unique qualities of their way of life.

This theory was later projected on a grand scale by the Yale historian, David Potter, in his book *People of Plenty*. According to Potter:

[9] Pierson, "The M–Factor in American History," *The American Quarterly*, pp. 275–89, Vol. XIV, Summer 1962 Supplement. © 1962 by American Quarterly Press.

Throughout our national experience, the most varied types of observers have agreed in emphasizing America's bounty. Explorers have marveled at wealth previously undiscovered; travelers have contrasted the riches of America with the scarcity of the lands from which they came; millions of inhabitants of the Old World have responded as immigrants to the lure of the land of plenty, the land of promise, where they could "dwell like kings in fairyland, lords of the soil"; politicians have urged the voters to vote himself a farm or a check for thirty dollars every Thursday or an old age pension or a war bonus, in the confident assurance that the country can meet the draft; exploiters have parried demands for conservation by contending that the sources of our wealth are unlimited . . . .[10]

In defense of his view, Potter cites a reported statement of Franklin D. Roosevelt, that, if he could place one American book in the hands of every Russian, the volume of his choice would be a Sears, Roebuck catalogue.

To demonstrate the impact of "abundance" upon the American character, Potter developed an analysis of the conditions surrounding an American youth. "Abundance," states Potter, "has revolutionized the typical mode of the child's nourishment, provided a characteristic style of housing and clothing, given him a permissive atmosphere in which to mature, provided the child with younger parents, largely exempted him from economic responsibility within the family, and created optimum conditions for prolonging life." He also asserts that the presence and force of abundance are recognizable in the whole range of American experience, American ideals, and American institutions. Furthermore, Potter presented the Turner Thesis with a formidable challenge.

[10] Reprinted from *People of Plenty* (p. 80), by David M. Potter by permission of The University of Chicago Press, © 1962.

Turner did not recognize that the attraction of the frontier was simply as the most accessible form of abundance, and therefore he could not conceive that other forms of abundance might replace it as the lodestone to which the needle of American aspirations would point. To him the frontier remained the polar force until it was exhausted . . . . Yet, in fact, what happened was that, as early as the mid-century, if not earlier, American industrial growth, relying upon the use of other forms of abundance than soil fertility, began to compete with the frontier in the opportunities which it offered, and the migration of Americans began to point to the cities rather than to the West . . . . In short, the frontier ceased to operate as a major force in American history not when it disappeared —not when the superintendent of the census abandoned the attempt to map a frontier boundary— but when the primary means of access to abundance passed from the frontier to other focuses in American life.[11]

Conclusion

In the extension and diffusion of culture, the frontiersman, in organized groups or as an individual wanderer, trader, colonist, or uprooted refugee, has been a primary agent. The culture of a new land could be fed from at least three sources: the region from which the frontiersman came, the components of that way of life he managed to bring with him and maintain, and the new environment that he entered. From ancient times to the present, scholars have given different weights to these varying factors, depending upon the basic sympathies of the writer and the type of frontier involved. Consequently, a pioneer may be pictured variously as a protector of old values such as Christianity,

[11] *Ibid.*, pp. 158–60.

as a creator of new institutions such as democratic government, or as a destroyer of old ways of life to make way for progress. Hence, the description of a national character has come to rest largely upon the particular perspective of each author.

Bibliography

Brogan, D. W.	*The American Character* Alfred A. Knopf, New York, N.Y.	1956 ed.
Bryce, James	*The American Commonwealth* Putnam & Sons, New York, N.Y.	1959 ed.
Commager, Henry	*The American Mind* Yale University Press, New Haven, Conn.	1959 ed.
De Tocqueville, Alexis	*Democracy in America* Mentor Books, New York, N.Y.	1956 ed.
Parkes, Henry	*The American Experience* Alfred A. Knopf, New York, N.Y.	1959 ed.
Parrington, Vernon L.	*Main Currents in American Thought,* Vols. I & II Harcourt, Brace & World, New York, N. Y.	1954 ed.
Potter, David	*People of Plenty* University of Chicago Press, Chicago, Ill.	1962 ed.
Wright, Benjamin	"Political Institutions and the Frontier," in *Sources of Culture in the Middle West,* Dixon Ryan Fox, ed., Appleton-Century-Crofts, New York, N.Y.	1934 ed.

Periodicals

Hacker, Louis	"Sections or Classes" *The Nation,* No. 187	July 26, 1933
Pierson, George	"The Frontier and American Institutions" *New England Quarterly,* No. 15	June, 1942
Pierson, George	"The M-Factor in American History" *The American Quarterly,* Vol. XIV, summer supplement	1962

INDEX

235

INDEX

ABOUT THE AUTHORS

D. Duane Cummins, a member of the faculty of Oklahoma City University, brings to this text his experience as one of the pioneer developers of "team teaching" "in-depth," and "inductive" approaches to the teaching of United States history.

He has taught American history at the secondary level for ten years in the Jefferson County Public School of Denver, Colorado and has served as Chairman of the Department of History for eight years.

Mr. Cummins has authored and co-authored a number of curriculum guides, was editor of American history overhead transparencies for Keuffel & Esser Co., and was a member of the writing staff of Educational Services, Inc., Boston.

Mr. Cummins, a member of the leading national historical associations, has been cited in the 1965 edition of *Outstanding Young Men in America.*

A native of Nebraska, he received a B.A. from Phillips University (Oklahoma), and an M.A. in American History from the University of Denver.

Co-author **William Gee White,** Chairman of the Social Studies Department at Arvada West High School, Colorado, has organized an in-depth program in American history and World history.

His teaching career, which began in 1953, has included assignments at primary and secondary levels in the Jefferson County, Colorado, Public School. He received the Classroom Teacher's Award of the Freedoms Foundation at Valley Forge.

Mr. White has participated in the writing program sponsored by the Committee on the Study of History, conducted at Amherst College, and is a member of the Western History Association and State Historical Society of Colorado.

A native of Colorado, he received a B.A. in Social Studies and an M.A. in American History from Colorado State College.

UNITED STATES HISTORY
by
D. Duane Cummins
William Gee White

In addition to *The American Frontier,* there are eight other paperbacks in this program. Each is an in-depth narrative of an important American experience which has left enduring effects on our national character.

Students can now get to know the real heroes of American history through the extensive quotations from diaries, journals, letters and speeches written "on-the-spot." They can interpret for themselves the real history of our country through this written heritage of opposing views, and from the contrasting interpretations of noted historians.

To guide the student in his role as "investigator," the respective teacher's manual contains correlated inductive exercises. It is also a resource book for the teacher, which illustrates how he can develop his own curriculum by interchanging chapters from all nine volumes, to meet the new scholarship demands and the needs of the different ability levels of his students.

OUR COLONIAL HERITAGE—discovering our heritage from the two oldest colonies—Virginia and Massachusetts.

THE AMERICAN REVOLUTION—examining the incidents that led to the conflicts which exploded into a revolution and independence, and interpreting these facts through the concept and pattern of revolution in our western civilization.

THE FEDERAL PERIOD—understanding our present two-party political system through events from 1789 to 1800, given from the viewpoints of the Federalists, and the Republicans.

ORIGINS OF THE CIVIL WAR—investigating the recognized causes of the war. Contains extensive material for the student to draw his own conclusions.

INDUSTRIALISM: THE AMERICAN EXPERIENCE—studying the problems of conversion from an agrarian society to an industrial society with emphasis on urbanization.

AMERICAN FOREIGN POLICY—re-living the United States' role in foreign affairs since 1789, stressing the instruments and agencies of foreign policy.

CONTRASTING DECADES: THE 20's AND THE 30's—comparing: depression and prosperity, laissez faire and central control, normalcy and reform, rural and urban values, Coolidge and Roosevelt.

DOMESTIC AMERICA SINCE 1950—going behind the headlines of our present-day conflicts such as affluence and want, conservatism and liberalism—and the race revolution.

This book was set in 10 point Times Roman by The Colonial Press Inc., Clinton, Mass., and printed on 60 lb. Light Natural paper. It was also printed and bound by The Colonial Press Inc. Cover and book design by Connie Urgo-Avon.

2008

2005